Praise for *If You Sit Very S...*

We are spared no aspect of the anguish, confusion and anger
experienced, but are also told an extraordinary story of inner
movement and growth – growth in a faith much less orthodox
on the face of it than Lucy's ardent Catholicism but equally deep
and serious. It is a book about the massive difficulty of anything
like reconciliation in the wake of outrage. There is nothing easily
consoling here, but rather a sense of stillness, acceptance and
hope – both given and worked for.
Rowan Williams, Book of the Year 2012,
Times Literary Supplement

There is not a sentence in this book that has not been felt, fought
for and hard won.
Craig Brown, Book of the Week,
The Mail on Sunday

This is not a story of "coping with loss", nor of "overcoming
emotion" nor less of "achieving forgiveness". It is the story of
simply, doggedly and patiently refusing to accept the path of
victimhood, revenge or bitter resentment. Instead Marian has
walked the way of uncertainty, humility and hope which, through
spiritual struggle and human kindness, accepts and transforms
sadness, loss and evil.
Stephen Cherry, author of
Healing Agony: Re-Imagining Forgiveness

Marian Partington's response to the pain, called by some the price
of love, is simply to open her heart with great honesty. If You Sit
Very Still should feature on everybody's bookshelf alongside such
life guides as Shakespeare and the Bible.
Jeffery Taylor, The Sunday Express

The heights and depths of what it means to be human are laid bare here. An inspiring, powerful testimony that bears witness to the human search for meaning and shows a generosity of spirit that grips heart and mind.
Ursula King, author of *The Search for Spirituality: Our Global Quest for Meaning and Fulfilment*

This book is beyond praise. It is a profound testament to how horrific evil and suffering can transform into redemptive forgiveness and healing. I read it straight through – I could not stop reading – and was moved to tears many times. Thank you, Marian Partington, for sharing your story with us.
David Loy, author of *Money, Sex, War, Karma*

Marian has given her sister's story a noble ending.
Deborah Orr, *Psychologies*

Lyrical, redemptive narrative.
Cathy Galvin, *Financial Times*

True forgiveness is a process; it requires dogged determination, ruthless honesty and tremendous hard work. In this immensely moving account of forgiveness and healing, and in language of great poetic and lyrical force, Marian Partington offers us something quite rare: the opportunity to make sense out of seemingly senseless brutality and violence and to understand the multiple layers of trauma they engender.
Jan Willis, author of *Dreaming Me: Black, Baptist and Buddhist – One Woman's Spiritual Journey*

If You Sit Very Still raises questions about the place of justice; whether it is true that all who cannot forgive necessarily become embittered; and whether evil can only be understood by looking inside ourselves. But, most important, it is about discarding the cloak of victimhood, so tempting to don, and, in a very literal sense, learning how to offer one's suffering for others.
Terry Philpot, *The Tablet*

If
You
Sit
Very
Still

of related interest

The Forgiveness Project
Stories for a Vengeful Age
Marina Cantacuzino
Forewords by Archbishop Emeritus Desmond
Tutu and Alexander McCall Smith
ISBN 978 1 84905 566 6 (hardback)
ISBN 978 1 78592 000 4 (paperback)
eISBN 978 1 78450 006 1

If
You
Sit
Very
Still

Marian Partington

Foreword by Marina Cantacuzino

Jessica Kingsley *Publishers*
London and Philadelphia

'I Hung a Poem on a Branch' by Yevgeny Yevtushenko, translated by George Reavey, is taken from *Early Poems* by Yevgeny Yevtushenko, Marion Boyars, 1969, 2009, and is reprinted with kind permission of Marion Boyars Publishers. 'Especially When it Snows' by Adrian Mitchell is taken from *Blue Coffee* by Adrian Mitchell, Bloodaxe Books, 1997, and is reprinted with kind permission of United Agents on behalf of Adrian Mitchell. The author's correspondence with Fergal Keane is reprinted with his kind permission.

First published in hardback edition by Vala Publishing Co-operative Ltd, UK in 2012
This edition first published in 2016
by Jessica Kingsley Publishers
73 Collier Street
London N1 9BE, UK
and
400 Market Street, Suite 400
Philadelphia, PA 19106, USA

www.jkp.com

Library of Congress Cataloging in Publication Data
A CIP catalog record for this book is available from the Library of Congress

British Library Cataloguing in Publication Data
A CIP catalogue record for this book is available from the British Library

ISBN 978 1 78592 140 7
eISBN 978 1 78450 407 6

Printed and bound in Great Britain

Preface

Written by the author for this paperback edition

Before the hardback edition of this book came out, I had been hoping, when people asked me about "my story", that I could say, "just read the book". I had imagined that maybe it would get on with its own life in the world, and leave me to get on with mine. But it hasn't seemed to work like that. It has continued to lead me into audiences and conversations beyond an invisible readership, beyond my comfort zone. There have been the interviews with book reviewers, the radio interviews (I didn't sleep a wink the night before Midweek with Libby Purves) and the Literary Festivals (Oxford, Cheltenham, Durham and Bloxham), along with my continuing work in prisons as a story teller and facilitator with the Forgiveness Project.

On one occasion, a few weeks after publication, in May 2012, I was taken to the crux of the matter. I had been invited to talk at "Hay in the Parc" – a collaboration between The Hay Festival and HMP Parc near Bridgend. I found myself sitting in a small room on the Vulnerable Prisoners Wing. The walls of the room were covered with sickening charts connected with the Sex Offenders

Treatment Programme (SOTP). Silent, subdued men began to fill the seats, avoiding my gaze. I felt overwhelmed. How could I go on with this? At the last minute a woman joined them. With a dry mouth I began to speak and read from the book. As I did, the atmosphere began to change. I looked up and saw the effect of the words. Somehow we were becoming human beyond our labels and prejudice.

I knew the truth of one prison officer's words:

> Your prison work is enabling criminals to look at the way they have behaved in a way that anyone not having your experience could not.

A few days later I received a card from the woman who had come in at the last minute, who was a member of the SOTP team:

> Working with people who commit sexual offences can be at times a very "dark place" where offences roll into one another and sadly so do the victims. To say the least you become "harder" to the world and "detach" from your feelings. Listening to you that afternoon filled me with sadness and for the first time in a long time I was able to cry, and continued to cry that evening and for that I want to thank you. I am glad I got to know who your sister was, what she liked...I purchased your book and read it in two days, my Mum is now reading it. It has made me realise again the importance of "our" role as the SOTP treatment team in helping towards making the world safer.

Many people have been affected by the book. Some say they couldn't put it down; others that they treated is as a precious gift and needed to wait for the right moment before they began. Some were affected by its very beauty and being:

> I don't know why but I was driven to handle the book with care as though in some way it was part of Lucy herself. She may not be here in person but she certainly lives through your beautiful book.

It feels good we have now included a photo of Lucy and me in the body of the book – an omission, first time around.

The book has inspired hope and been described as "an education of the spirit". It has brought comfort, inspiration and healing.

Sometimes I wonder how I wrote it. But then I remember what compelled me and how I gave as much time as was needed (eighteen years) to allow the right words and the right shape to emerge. It feels true, as someone said, that Lucy had a hand in it.

And, yes, the book continues to stretch my spirit and challenge me to grow closer to understanding and living the truth of these words:

> *If we are all part of each other, even beyond our ...*
> *breathing out for the last time from this body, then to*
> *withhold compassion towards any form of life lessens*
> *our true place of belonging and destroys our potential*
> *community.* (see page 140)

May this paperback edition continue to confront and dissolve the roots of fear and prejudice that lie within and without, and help to nourish and allow a more generous and loving world.

Marian Partington
Victoria BC, Canada
1st February 2015

Foreword

I first met Marian Partington just a few weeks after the start of the Iraq war, in 2003. At a time when the whole world was talking about retaliation, I was trying to collect stories from people who had considered forgiveness in the face of atrocity. I had been told by a friend about Marian's remarkable journey of healing following the kidnap and brutal murder of her younger sister, Lucy, at the hands of serial killers Frederick and Rosemary West. I wanted to find out how anyone could line themselves up for forgiveness following an event of such unspeakable savagery. It was an important and pivotal moment for me. It was only after hearing Marian's story that I realised that the ethos behind my own project could never simply be to present inspiring stories which drew a line under the dogma of vengeance, but rather must provide a place of inquiry for people to explore the limits and complexities of forgiveness.

I subsequently distilled our intense, four hour discussion into a short, first-person testimony which, together with a stirring portrait of Marian, went on display alongside twenty-six other stories in an exhibition at the Oxo Gallery in London in 2004. I called the exhibition *The F Word* because by then I knew that forgiveness was a messy business; it was something which no one could agree on and seemed to inspire and affront in equal measure. Marian's story of moving through murderous rage to a place of understanding and compassion made me realise that forgiveness should never be sanitised or glorified, that it was difficult, painful and costly, but also that it could be the crucial ingredient in transforming deep and unresolved pain.

Since that time I have been privileged to witness Marian sharing her story with numerous people in many settings, but mostly in adult male prisons, including in one sex offenders' wing. It is always a profound experience, to watch her telling her story to men who have harmed others. Invariably, and in an astonishingly short time, fixed perceptions start to shift, hardened attitudes soften, and even the most resistant begin to unbend.

Above all, it is when Marian brings out the little, woollen, hand-spun bag, carefully woven from stray sheep's wool by her sister when she was eight, and passes it around the group, that the mood settles in the room. It has always struck me that allowing countless strangers, one after the other, session after session, to handle and hold in the palm of their hands this most precious and delicate of gifts is an extraordinary gesture of generosity. By trusting these men with an object invested with so much emotional value, Marian transforms this story of hell into a message of hope.

I read *If You Sit Very Still* over one twenty-four hour period. I was mesmerised by the language and gripped not only by the need to know what happened next, but also by the desire to understand how anyone can truly reconcile with such evil. You feel that you have been taken by the hand, led gently along a terrifying path (which few will mercifully know) into previously uncharted territory, and allowed to share in this deeply personal chronicle of grief.

Emerging through trauma, pain and finally towards transformation, the author seeks to explain and give voice to a humanity born out of intense sorrow. She repeatedly and painstakingly searches for and then grasps the exact word or expression to faithfully describe every step of the journey until a new narrative emerges. This is a journey towards becoming forgiving – the only creative route Marian could find to soothe and mend her broken world. There were times I stopped to read and re-read the words as they unfolded on the page, in awe of her ability to explain the inexplicable, give meaning to the incomprehensible and describe such deep agony through the towering lyricism of her prose. The great accomplishment of this narrative of healing is its capacity to uncover the gift in the wound which, to paraphrase W. B. Yeats, permits "a terrible beauty" to be born.

Marina Cantacuzino
Founder and Director of The Forgiveness Project
www.theforgivenessproject.com

In memory of dear Lucy

For David and Mark, my brothers,
and Margaret and Roger, our parents

With a love that continues

Deepening

For all

Contents

Prologue

Lucy Partington was my sister, four years younger than me. On 27th December 1973 she left her friend Helen's house in time to walk to the bus stop in Evesham Road, Cheltenham, intending to catch the 10.15 p.m. bus back to our home in Gretton. She didn't catch the bus. She was twenty-one years old and in her final year of an English degree at Exeter University. She was reported missing and a national search was launched. She became one of thousands of "missing people", for twenty years.

On 4th March (her birthday) 1994 Frederick West told the investigation team in Gloucester that there were more bodies in the basement of 25 Cromwell Street and one of them was Lucy's. For those readers who were around in the UK at that time this crime will need no introduction. For those who weren't, Frederick and Rosemary West ("the Wests") were responsible for the rape, torture and murder of twelve young women (and possibly more) between 1971 and 1987.

To say "My sister was murdered, she was one of the Wests' victims" makes my throat ache. It was easier to say "My sister disappeared", but more difficult to live with that sense of

1

unresolved loss. However, the grotesque details surrounding Lucy's death are part of my life. It is not possible to pretend it didn't happen. It is hardly possible to understand. But there is something about trying to get the measure of it before one can let go of it. It is vast and slippery. It is sticky and staining. It is the distance to be walked in the shaping of this book.

We can never know exactly what took place. Most of Lucy's bones, her poetry and something of her spirit survived. We will never know how she coped with what must be one of the worst possible ways to die. But let us not forget that many women, children and men are violently abused and killed in the context of war, domestic violence and random murder every day.

The book that Lucy carried in her bag the night that she was abducted was also stolen and never returned. It was a fourteenth-century Dream Vision called *Pearl*.[1] We had both studied it as part of our English Literature degrees.

The words of the *Pearl* manuscript were written before electricity and printing. Each letter poured off the end of a feather plucked from the skin of a goose or a swan, shaped for the flow of ink, the stroke of stem on parchment. The hole in the parchment, where the leg of the goat would have been severed from the skin, was stitched into a rough scar on the page, interrupting the flow of letters. Goose and goat were sacrificed for the script, the illumination. The scribe did not know that his exquisite words would be with you, Lucy, in your bag, the night you were abducted. They had travelled for seven hundred years.

The poem is uncannily, almost unbelievably, appropriate to Lucy's nature and fate, as well as to my mental and spiritual journey. It is as if its being there were trying to tell me something. While researching medieval dream visions in the National Library of Wales I read that this genre is "a process of psychic redemption, closely resembling, though wider in scope than, modern psychotherapy."[2] Piehler described the shape of the medieval dream vision as: 1) Crisis 2) Confession 3) Comprehension 4) Transformation.

If You Sit Very Still echoes this structure, although I have changed the nouns to verbs to indicate that this quest is a continuing, fluctuating process that cannot be ticked off with the static completion of nouns. The sections overlap and are dependent upon each other. It is also in four parts, with the addition of a Prologue and an Epilogue: Crisis, Confessing, Comprehending and Transforming. It is a narrative of healing, a movement towards becoming forgiving, which attempts to remain true to an uncharted, incomplete process.

CRISIS

Pearl begins with the crisis of a father's grief. He is lamenting the loss of his precious, singularly perfect "Pearl" in the premature death of a pure maiden or young child. He is grieving in a garden where "he lost her", grovelling on her grave. The all-consuming physical immediacy of his grief "swells" and "burns" within his heart. He can only fall onto the earth of the grave mound, where he is overwhelmed by a sudden sleep. Disorientated, he finds himself in a dream vision where "marvels meven" (marvels move). He wanders on the edge of a jewelled landscape of dazzling purity on the other side of a river. In this dream world, he feels a temporary cure from the physical pain of his grief, as he wanders along the bank, allowing his senses to be soothed and amazed.

The first section of this book explores my experience of the disappearance for twenty years of my sister Lucy and the traumatic effect of the discovery of her remains in Gloucester. Much ground was covered in this time of searching for our "lost Pearl". It was a time of prolonged dislocation. The lack of a grave kept us suspended. We had to carry on living. But for me there was also the focus of the first two dreams that came to me, marking and informing the beginning and end of the twenty years of Not Knowing, and offering a broader, deeper location within the river that flows beyond life and death.

CONFESSING

A young maiden arrayed with pearls appears in the shining paradise on the other side of the river and approaches the Dreamer. He experiences dread, bliss and inadequacy, his pride trusting only what his intelligence perceives. Gradually he recognises his lost pearl – but her identity is no longer clear. There is a dialogue between them. The Pearl Maiden begins to confront his human ignorance. She challenges his isolating attitude of contempt and leads him, gradually, to confess and acknowledge his stubborn arrogance and self-centred grief.

The second section of this book slowly begins to unravel my own history and experience of that which was in the way of moving towards the acceptance and integration of the complex loss of Lucy. It became vital to face and acknowledge (confess) the darkness within me, the roots of my murderous rage, and then to find my voice and speak out (profess), as the frozen silence within me began to thaw. I relate the process of finding words that came from an unavoidable, passionate need to reclaim Lucy from the Wests and the media, to free her from the labels in the public domain ("missing person", "West victim"). My first account of this experience was an essay, *Salvaging the Sacred*, published in *The Guardian Weekend* in May 1996, and later (in 2004) as a Quaker Books pamphlet.[3] The book that you are reading is grounded in its words.

COMPREHENDING
The third step for the Pearl Dreamer is to comprehend that only by continuing to excavate the layers of unresolved pain can he be realigned in order to know his "kynde", the pure-hearted, well-wishing, loving kindness within him, which leads him, naturally, towards unity with all things. This is his true nature, released from afflictive emotions, "unspotted" (clear, unblemished, unclouded). The theological dialogue with the Pearl Maiden continues as she leads him towards acceptance. She tries to teach him, with a blunt directness reminiscent of a Zen mistress, that he must let go of his imprisoning, self-centred emotions and surrender to the unique meaning of his own life. The Dreamer continues to struggle and resist. He comprehends his inadequacy, and his need for mercy and grace (his mind is trapped in the earthly "dungeon's blight"). He begins to soften and listen. He knows a moment of freedom and eternity when he glimpses the New Jerusalem, "a symbol of home-coming, of safety and haven, of fulfilment and fruitfulness, of permanence and purity, of colour and light".[4]

The third section of this book continues my inner quest towards knowing my "kynde" through a gradual dissolving of that which was in the way. This radical self-investigation was enabled, in part, by regular Chan (Chinese Zen) Buddhist retreats, and through the discipline and silent, contemplative prayer of Quaker faith and practice. The narrative of this excavation moves towards a way of comprehending and an acceptance of that which is beyond comprehension. The elusive, worn-out noun, "forgiveness", springs to life as an ongoing verb, *"for-giving"*.

TRANSFORMING

The Pearl Dreamer eventually begins to accept his loss and the changed identity of his "lost pearl". But in a rash, impetuous moment he longs to cross to the other side of the river (die) to join her. That irrational desire jerks him out of his dream. However, he recognises that he has begun to experience the transformation of his personal loss into a place of metaphysical, universal meaning, even if his impatient longing has returned him to the cold earth of the temporal grave. During the dialogue in the dream vision his grief has changed. He has glimpsed the eternal unity of all forms of life and been humbled.

The last section of the book explores the ripening of my inner work and its turning outwards into a transforming engagement with the world of restorative justice over a period of ten years. I connect with those who have committed serious crimes, sharing something of this ongoing narrative of healing and reconciliation, and its effect upon others. The final chapter explores the transformative power of words and an attempt to reach out towards Rosemary West through writing a letter to her.

At the beginning of these travels into the uncharted territory of traumatic loss, I had come across these words in a book by the Dalai Lama:

> *I will learn to cherish beings of bad nature*
> *And those pressed by strong sins and suffering*
> *As if I had found a precious*
> *Treasure very difficult to find*[5]

I know Lucy would have understood their meaning. "Love your enemies and pray for those who persecute you."[6] Through my own experience, I am slowly coming to understand them myself.

Lucy, four months after you disappeared I had the first dream. You had returned and I asked you where you had been. You said, "I've been sitting in a water meadow near Grantham." Then slowly, with a smile, you said,

If you sit very still you can hear the sun move.

This image filled me with a profound feeling of peace, the kind that "passeth understanding". This feeling remained with me when waking. It lasted for a few seconds. It has remained deeply significant, and real. Did you speak to me from there? When he was three years old, my son Jack came into our bed one morning and said, "You know that dream we had last night…" He then told me in great detail about "our" dream. I wonder, is there a place where we all share the same dream? Is that the place where what has been dismembered can be remembered? Is it the place where you can hear the sun move?

This dream reminds me of the tone of your voice, Lucy. It has burned at the core of my spiritual quest.

Dear reader, I offer these "spotted" words in the hope that you may remember your true "kynde".

Crisis

Chapter 1

DISAPPEARANCE

The crisis caused by Lucy's death was long. There are many theories about the short and long-term effects of trauma, many of them pessimistic. Yet the Chinese word for "crisis" has two meanings: "danger" and "opportunity for change". It is time to speak about my way through all this. It has been an extraordinary opportunity for change, a valuable chance to deepen my powers of compassion by facing the reality of my deepest fears, and that which has been buried within me. This is an attempt to find words and images to describe significant moments in my struggle to integrate that which is essentially beyond reason and, in many ways, beyond words.

But words must be found. There must be something for all of us to learn from the profoundly shocking profanity of the murder of Lucy, my sister, before it becomes buried under the concrete of fear, prejudice, or even worse, indifference. This speaking is about Lucy's truth, in her life and in her death. It is about trying to remain open to the pain, the guilt, the joy, the rage, the grief, the fear and what lies beyond. It is about my quest to find meaning. It is about living with the reality of violence, rape, torture and murder, trying to face up to it and trying to accept it. It is about poetry and transformation. The process is not always rational. It is about learning to follow my heart. It is a rite of passage. It is purgatorial. It is about time. The process is about "Salvaging the Sacred" – the sacred in my sister, in myself and, ultimately, in all sentient beings.

Lucy was lucky to come from a family who loved her. We are led to believe that the majority of the young women in the West case were not so fortunate. "They" managed to get lost without many people noticing or searching. "They" did not have much of a sense of purpose or direction in their lives. "They" have been labelled "natural victims". Every one of the girls and young women in "the West Case" had a right to live: Heather West (1970-June 1987, first child of Fred and Rosemary West); Charmaine West (1963-1971, Fred's stepdaughter, daughter of Rena Costello); Lynda Gough (1953-April 1973, lodger); Juanita Mott (1957-April 1975, former lodger); Therese Siegenthaler (1952-April 1974, student from London hitchhiking to Ireland); Shirley Hubbard (1959-November 1974, walking home in Droitwich); Carol Ann Cooper (1958-November 1973, walking back to a children's home in Worcester); Alison Chambers (1962-August 1979, from Swansea, living in Gloucester); Shirley Ann Robinson (1959-May 1978, lodger, Fred's lover, pregnant); Rena Costello (1944-1971, Fred's first wife, Charmaine's mother); Ann Mcfall (Rena's friend, Fred's lover, pregnant). Their lives had equal value to Lucy's.

That Christmas of 1973, three of us had come back to The Mill (our family home in Gretton, Gloucestershire) for the holiday period. Mark, our youngest brother, who was in his final year in the 6th form, had not yet left home. 28th December, the day after Lucy disappeared, was the Feast of the Holy Innocents, as one of Lucy's Catholic friends pointed out. This was Lucy's first Christmas as a Catholic. She had been received into the Catholic Church five weeks earlier at the Chaplaincy at Exeter University.

My boyfriend Patrick and I returned from a night away with local friends in Stroud. Mum rushed out into the drive with a voice full of panic. "Lucy didn't come home last night." Dave, one of my two brothers, seemed particularly agitated, cursing that he would kill anyone who had harmed her. "If anyone has laid a hand on her I'll fucking kill them!" It was clear that something terrible had happened. The police came, eventually, having brushed our concern aside at first with their idea that it was just after Christmas and she had probably gone off with her boyfriend. When they came to our home and talked to us, they realised that she was unlikely to be so irresponsible.

Dad came down from Hutton Rudby, in Yorkshire, and sat on the sofa holding Mum's hand. My brother Mark said "You had to come didn't you?" It was the first time our parents had seen each other since the divorce eleven years earlier. Dad stayed down the road with a neighbour and helped the police with their search.

"Missing Person" posters were stuck up on trees around Cheltenham, and road-blocks and interviews were set up. The investigation room was kept open for seven years. Did the Wests read the newspaper reports during the national search, and see her photograph stuck to trees and walls? We searched for her, desperately. We lost her for twenty years. How many people knew where she was but didn't say anything? Facing what we lost, speaking about what we lost, is necessary but wrenching. It causes a strangling, gripping pain in my throat and chest.

Lucy, when you went out into the public domain on all those posters pinned to trees as a "Missing Person" I couldn't breathe a sigh of relief. Part of my breath was held back. My respiration became less vital. Part of my reality had gone missing too. Sometimes it felt as if I were going mad. In this state, you scan horizons, corners, streets, shops. You can't switch off. Your concentration is eroded into permanent restlessness. You just need to know where the missing person is.

My brother Dave said he used to think sometimes he had seen you, passing by on an escalator in the underground, or just going around a corner. Other friends have described this feeling of being on constant lookout for Lucy. Yet we all had to go on living our lives. Every day you try to remember the person, you battle against the passing of time that threatens to disintegrate your memory. There are days when you are suffocated by glutinous guilt the moment you realise that you haven't thought about the person for a while, that you have given up looking, that you are dragging around a hole that can't be filled. This sense of loss cannot fail to disable you. If you deny it, it grows even bigger and slashes its way back.

Lucy had kindness, sensitivity, humour, warmth and a piercing intelligence. These qualities seem to shine out of the photograph that was posted everywhere. It was taken in the summer of 1973 by our father during a visit to him in Yorkshire. We were at Rievaulx Abbey, in Yorkshire. It was the last time Lucy and I spent time together on our own with Dad. Lucy had me labelled as an Incorrigible Romantic. She teased me, accusing me of being a bit Undisciplined and prone to Flights of Fancy and Imagination. My retort was that she was being a bit on the Classical side, preferring a Clear Structure and lots of Discipline. We talked at length about our parents and tried to understand why they had divorced. We were beginning to re-form and deepen our relationship. She worried about my hitchhiking everywhere. It was certainly a huge part of my survivor's guilt that she was so against hitching and that I did it all the time. This is the "it should have been me" syndrome, that most siblings and friends suffer for a while.

Lucy tended to do the opposite of those around her. She was renowned for being sensible. She protected her vulnerability with an acerbic wit and an ability to be witheringly critical. Her attitude to me seemed to be a mixture of disapproval and admiration. She was confused and threatened by my "predictable" exploration of Flower Power and fashion, and was possibly ashamed that I was "on the pill" and living with my boyfriend. But at Rievaulx Abbey she had stopped needing to keep me at arm's length. The difference between us was no longer threatening. We had begun to appreciate each other's company and develop a mutual respect.

In November 1973 Lucy was received into the Catholic Church. It was a courageous step to take, coming as she did from an agnostic background (although our great-grand-parents were involved in the Chinese Inland Mission). Her faith was fresh and real.

In 1973 she wrote to a friend, Pat:

> *The most important thing I have done this year, and what if I could have foreseen it two years ago I would have considered nothing short of insanity, is to become a Catholic. Don't worry, I didn't have a vision or anything. In fact, I must be one of the most unspectacular subjects in the history of conversions, and I'm sure I felt more embarrassment than spiritual illumination. Another more refined form of embarrassment is that, intellectually, it's such a predictable thing to do…Father Hay, the University Chaplain, is instructing me, and a finer balance of intellectualism, piety, and irreverence you couldn't care to meet anywhere. He really is lovely. My friends and relations etc. think it's all a huge joke, and it's really much easier than I ever thought.*

In a letter written to a friend dated 1st June 1973 from Upton Pyne near Exeter she wrote:

> *I think I have changed quite a lot in the last few months, not fundamentally, but in the way of a general softening up of sharp edges, and being more accepting.*

She spoke about her Catholicism:

> *although I still can't bear the idea of being a convert, I'm extremely happy about it and can't think why I didn't do something about it sooner.*

In the same letter she spoke of one of her tutors:

> *one of his poems, which for some reason incorporates a lot of American Jazz idiom ends:*

> > *stick around, puss-cats*
> > *we're all in this together*

> *and has almost become the motto of the medieval department. I frequently mutter it to myself as I bicycle dangerously along the New North Road.*

Her reference to inter-connectedness ("we're all in this together") would prove to be prophetic, as would her reference, later in the letter, to change resulting from communication, in the "medieval group" which

has, from being such unpromising material, as I thought, turned into a very friendly company.

Her tutors regarded Lucy as on target to receive a First Class honours degree. She wrote about the impending Finals (which she never had the opportunity to take):

The most enjoyable literature studies have been the lyric and the romance, and almost all the art has been good. We went on a field trip to the Gloucester area for a weekend, and I was amazed how much we had absorbed, and could apply.

By the first of several horrible twists of fate, the field trip included a visit to the Church of St Bartholomew in Much Marcle, where Fred West grew up.

Five weeks after her reception into the Catholic Church she suffered a death that exceeded our worst imaginings. Are there any words that can hold the pain of that collision? Is there any language with which she could have appealed, if her mouth, her voice, had not been gagged? Her moral status was an integral part of her identity in a way that was clear and fully intact. Her sexual status was innocent. Her spiritual status was both inspiring and aspiring towards perfection. Was she simply, heartbreakingly, unlucky?

It was impossible not to ask her priest, Monsignor George Hay (who is still alive) if he thought that Lucy's faith would have helped her in her terrifying ordeal. This was one of those unanswerable questions in the league of "why did it happen to Lucy?" and "was it really as random as 'She Was In The Wrong Place At The Wrong Time'"? He meditated quietly for a while and said, "Well it's just a feeling I have, but I do feel that she would have maintained her integrity." Knowing Lucy's intellectual and spiritual refinement, it was mostly possible to believe that and to pray that her faith gave her strength, maybe even understanding and acceptance of the apparently incomprehensible and unacceptable.

Lucy, just before you disappeared, we were exploring the questions that arise on the threshold to adulthood about our similar roots: our shared childhood, and our shared genes. It struck me as deeply significant that you had been murdered five weeks after you were received into the Catholic Church, and that we found out nearly twenty one years later, five weeks after I had been accepted as a member of the Religious Society of Friends (Quakers). My daughter had chosen to be christened in the Anglican Church (Church in Wales) when she was nine. Supporting my daughter's choice had led me to explore the Quaker faith as an attender at Quaker Meetings for Worship for seven years. Their liturgy is silence. We had each chosen to deepen our commitment to apparently opposite religious faiths and communities (in their outward form, but not in their approach to divine mystery and revelation) and five weeks later we each faced an extreme crisis.

Sadly, we didn't have time to explore together the meaning of your religious commitment. Your Catholic friends assure me that even if you couldn't pray when you were dying (a question that plagued me for a while), you were being prayed for by the Communion of Saints. It is a comforting idea to imagine a host of invisible saints sustaining an eternal loop of prayer somewhere or other.

We all speculated, mostly privately, about why you had disappeared. Perhaps there were various strains that you were subjected to that might have made you severely depressed. You had to sleep in a bedroom with a thin straw partition listening to Patrick Murphy (my boyfriend at the time) and me (on the pill) sinning away, unmarried, conforming to the age of Sexual Liberation. Patrick prided himself upon being a lapsed Catholic. But you did like Patrick. Somehow he met with your approval, maybe because he offered to help more with the cooking and washing-up than the rest of us. You hadn't come across a male in our generation who liked cooking and was good at it (nor had I). He made excellent pizzas, and showed you how to make the dough from *The Tassajara Bread Book*. He had a good sense of humour and was particularly good at Irish-accented mockery of his Catholic ancestry. Shortly before you vanished he had been gently teasing you about your recent conversion to Catholicism. In fact, you were quite capable of mocking your own need for the certainties of the Church. Once, you wrote:

> *p.s. talking of wanting to work in a cathedral, I no sooner discovered the other day, that the Inns of Court were still in existence, than I had a desire to become a lawyer – obvious need to belong to some exclusive and tradition ridden organisation.*

Maybe our behaviour made you depressed in the light of your recent conversion?

You were going off to visit our father the next morning. The attempt to please both parents, and take presents on our behalf, was another strain. Maybe you were anxious about that? You were "not yourself", according to your friend Helen's statement, although she couldn't say why. When you left Helen's home in Cheltenham to catch the bus home, so that you could have an early night before the train journey to Hutton Rudby to visit Dad the next morning, you drew your logo next to the date on Helen's calendar. The logo was a moose's head. "Luce the Moose" was your self-appointed nickname. That evening you signed your logo with the mouth turned down. That was unlike your usual ebullience, so apparent in this poem to your friend.

To Helen
Hail <u>Helena</u>! Who alone hast borne
Bright <u>Learnings</u> Torch, thro' <u>Mockery</u> & Scorn;
That sapient brow with Laurel-wreaths adorn,
(Or crocheted <u>Hat</u>) & never cease from morn
To Musk, blooming, ye <u>Roses</u>! <u>Lilies</u> all, bow down!
(A Skinny Ode, in which she pays tribute to her friend's
Genius Accomplishment, no less pleasant for being entirely
expected, containing many a subtle reference entirely Free
of Charge)
Lucy Partington

Helen died two years after your disappearance. Her parents joined with my mother in grief for a while.

Another thought was that you might have run off to join a nunnery. Of all the theories about what had happened to you, this was the most appealing because you would still be alive and you would be following your deepest needs. You were so unhappy with the decadence of the age that you needed to renounce the world. Your aspiration to purity and a relationship with God would be fulfilled. The fact that you didn't tell us about it was our fault because we were all too Undisciplined and Immoral. It would answer your need for security that we were unable to provide. It would be empowering for you. You could be free of us, we who deserved to be left in the lurch because we were so boorish and selfish.

We were told that it would not have been possible to join a closed order without the knowledge of your family. In any case, no, you would not have been that uncaring towards us poor sinners. Although religious fervour is responsible for all sorts of cruel, fanatical actions, it would not have been your way of doing things unless you had undergone a complete personality change. But if that was what you had done, we should wait for you to contact us, when you felt ready.

For a while the extraordinary fact that your priest (who was the Catholic Chaplain at Exeter University at the time) was in Cheltenham on the night of your disappearance, allowed that fantasy to take root.

The other scenario – that you had committed suicide – could be convincing, but was less acceptable because it meant that you were dead. You had drowned yourself in Pitville Lake. The lake was dragged. No body was found. The possibility of your suicide provided even more of a bonanza for our sense of guilt. There were various facts that could be accumulated to provide a convincing case for this event. You were feeling wobbly that evening. It was your first Christmas as a Catholic convert among your family who were blatantly sinners. You had told Norman at the farm, on Christmas morning, on your way to feed the horses, that we were "miles behind" in our preparation of the Christmas dinner. You had commented with approval that they were on schedule at the farm, despite the mammoth turkey (a twenty pounder, the prize pick of their breedings). You had already been to church with the Greenhows, the only other practising Catholics in the village. You despised our lack of discipline and lack of religious observance.

But your disappearance could not be fathomed. We have all been invaded and haunted by our own reconstructions of the gap between the bus stop and the archaeology of your dustbin grave. For me, the need to know the details is as instinctive as giving birth. My version goes like this. The Wests had been visiting Rosemary's parents in Bishops Cleeve. They saw you and turned back to ask if they could give you a lift. "Missed the bus my love?" The bus was late that night and you may have been worried about bothering the Renders (Helen's parents) for a lift. By yet another of the horrible twists of fate, you had declined the offer of a lift home from Helen's from Mum and my brother, who were also out visiting friends in Cheltenham that evening. All of us were out that evening with various friends. Dave was the last one of us to see you, when he dropped you off at Helen's. What did the Wests say to you? "Where are you going? Oh hop in then." Would you have thought it safe to go in a car with two friendly adults?

Not until 2010 did we learn that on her last evening in Devon, Lucy and a student friend had been sitting on the floor by a fire in the living room of one of their tutors, toasting pikelets, spreading them with honey, and discussing the friend's intention to hitchhike home. Lucy was characteristically appalled by the idea, but her tutor remarked "Well, I suppose it would be all right if there were a woman as well as a man in the car, especially if they had children with them." The tutor has agonised over that comment ever since. The woman in the fateful car was younger than you. She may have had a young child with her. Mum, however, can only imagine that you were forced into the car. David and Mark wouldn't talk about it. I was seen as "the odd one out" because I wanted to talk about it, although this did change with time.

When you disappeared, the police took dogs and searched every single church on the Department of English's long Gloucestershire and Herefordshire Field Trip itinerary, because you had been in each of them. They even scoured your letters for clues. Surely the police must have understood something of your personality when they read letters like this one, written in 1971 in semi-italic handwriting in black ink:

It's been very hot and heavy all morning and now the storm has broken and the thunder seems to start far away and roll right around the circle of the hills. Thank you Tennyson and shake the whole house. It's moving away now. I had to stop to watch the lightning—great forks coming out of the tops of the elm trees. I love thunderstorms. It came right overhead and it was like

> *Let Nature crush the sides of the earth together*
> *And mar the seeds within (Tennyson)*

I went for a walk after lunch through the old orchards and the beech wood above the house, which is more like paradise than anything Milton imagined. The pear trees are all heaped up with blossom and the grass is covered in cuckoo flowers and cowslips and violets and great beds of kingcups by the stream. I found a tiny pink flower, opening white, which I had never seen before. I looked it up and it's called "Lamb's Lettuce". You can't take a step in the wood without treading on bluebells which are out.

I have to inform you, Lucy, that the cowslip meadow in Gretton below the railway line is now planted with a bungalow, and it is illegal to pick wild flowers. All the elm trees have died from Dutch Elm Disease. The hedges on Gretton Hill, and the edge of the garden at The Mill where the rooks nested, rising and falling like a black net, filling the air with a cacophony of caws, have all changed. The stile that we used to climb over, on our way to the Parkers' Farm to fetch warm, yellow milk in our dented aluminium milk churn, is now a barbed wire fence. The elm tree stumps form the uprights. The year after you disappeared, the lane was filled with Bovis homes and leylandii. In the context of your death, the emphasis and syntax of the words that you left us have shifted and intensified in some way. The nightmare that you described in your letter of 15th June 1972, eighteen months before you were murdered, was prophetic:

I had a nightmare last night about an estate of bungalows and great banks of bare mud on which nothing would grow.

Your flesh was sealed in a clay hole beneath a layer of concrete. It could not feed the earth.

When Lucy was abducted, her satchel contained not only the book, *Pearl,* but also my last present to her. She had shown it to her friend Helen before leaving to catch the 10.15 p.m. bus that was never reached. It was a Victorian cut-glass jar, the right size to hold a night-light candle. It was the colour of amethyst, and could be hung on a Christmas tree or in a window by its wire handle, casting a soothing, pale-purple glow, redolent of sunlight shining through stained glass in a place of worship, as if meditative, or maybe the colour of the air at dawn, just before the sun appears. Lucy had been delighted with it, and talked of using it as her night-light when she was back in her hall of residence after the Christmas holiday. It was bought as part of a job lot in the Portobello Road. It was never recovered. (The police brought a strange green glass to The Mill which they had recovered during their investigation at 25 Cromwell Street. They thought that it might be the present described to them in 1974 after you disappeared. It looked like a souvenir from Weston-super-Mare.) The right word for its real colour came to me from medieval stained glass vocabulary. In the huge windows at the Tudor mansion, Hengrave Hall, it is the colour of Christ's robes as he kneels alone, praying in the garden of Gethsemane. The colour is called "murrey".

Also inside the bag was a letter of application to the Courtauld Institute of Art in London to take a postgraduate course in medieval art history. It was never posted.

All three objects in the satchel-bag were joyous parts of Lucy's future. I used to wonder what the Wests made of *Pearl*, of the night-light, and of the unposted letter. The gap of prejudice was intense in those days. It shocked me. The trenches were firmly dug in my mind. Nothing in "their" environment would be remotely like anything in "ours".

This is where, for me, it all goes into slow motion: the moment when Lucy, satchel-bag swinging on her shoulder, hurried through the darkest of nights, in the national power-cut owing to the fuel crisis, intending to post the letter before the bus came – the moment when Lucy's life met its opposite. Gargoyles came to life and destroyed her. Euphemisms serve to numb the senses and present the unpresentable. Maybe that is the best one can do.

No, try again; you are avoiding it. Put it into words. It is medieval hell. It smacks of concentration camps and nuclear bombs. Try to imagine the moment when she was abducted from her own direction in life and debased into a physical object to be treated as mere flesh and bones for the gratification of some other human beings whose quest was the opposite of hers. They didn't know the beauty of her soul. They stole her, gagged her, tied her up, toyed with her, raped her, tortured her, and at some unknown time, killed her or allowed her to die, slowly. They caused her unimaginable physical and emotional suffering. How long was she kept alive, unable to scream or struggle? Was it days, weeks, months?

Lucy, you had not died unfingered. Your flesh was cleaved, hacked and prodded by drooling fangs and flickering tongues of gargoyles. They guttered your body. Guttering, were you wrapped with grace? Could you pray? Words did not save you, Lucy, but words can raise the flesh of hope; they may save me. Who died when you were killed? How might your voice have been changed by your death? You had no voice from your mouth during your death. That is so hard for me to imagine – your having no words to express your outrage, your pain, your beauty, your wit, the poetry of your fretting soul, while all that was going on. You heard West's obscene language.

I can't remember the sound of your voice, Lucy. Now, after all this time, more than three decades, it is hard to remember the tones, the intonations, the inflections, the words that you would have chosen in your life, but the words that you left behind and that you send in dreams quicken me. You suffered unspeakable pain. Maybe your body in pain was your prayer – your crucifixion. It took me years to make this connection and write it down. It seemed almost sacrilegious to allow these thoughts.

They beheaded and dismembered her and stuffed her into a small hole, surrounded by leaking sewage pipes, head first, face down, still gagged. Her flesh decomposed into a tarry black slime that stained the clay walls of the hole and coated the bones. The rope that held her in bondage, two hair grips, a few strands of hair and the masking tape gag survived with most of her bones. Who knows what happened to the missing bones?

Lucy, your flesh was trashed. You could not feed the earth. Your death could not feed us because we could not bury you.

Chapter 2

THE NOT KNOWING

The early years for me, when I was 26 years old and you, Lucy, had just vanished and I was left to finish my degree without you, were blurred and numbed. It was a bit like the time after Dad left thirteen years before. We hadn't had the ritual, we hadn't had a funeral, everything was on hold and it was as if part of me was frozen, waiting, and I couldn't go on as a whole person.

The huge sense of loss with no opportunity to grieve properly certainly didn't lessen as the years went by. On an emotional level, both the fear that she had been murdered, and sometimes the hope that she was still alive, were kept at bay. One of the most painful aspects was the feeling that as a family we had never paid tribute to her life.

The subject became almost taboo. For some time it was impossible for me to imagine that she had been murdered, let alone talk about it. It was almost as if naming that possibility would be treading on a land mine. We had better not dare to rehearse that scene, because even putting it into words would be tempting fate. There was a strange process going on. The longer we didn't speak about what might have happened, the worse it felt. The hole of Not Knowing had its own drill-like momentum. It was becoming a deep pit, eroded by our not being able to share our feelings about it. The conspiracy of silence required a mutual adherence to an unspoken law. In our ignorant attempt to protect each other from pain, and deny our own feelings, we tried to carry on as if nothing had happened. We were becoming more isolated from each other. Our lives became "the story without Lucy".

Stuck as a fly in amber, no-one speaks, gagged into masked conformity. The pain no-one speaks about because there are no words or because the words will crack open the pain. The words would express the pain, share the pain. But it is taboo. Imaginings grow, expand, fed by what is unspeakable. The silence tries to hide the horror that rotted in a basement. If we don't say it, it might not be true. Life goes on, but only life that pretends, hides in the silence, that magnifies the pain. The taboo is against the pain of being alive. As Joseph Campbell said, "Love is the pain of being alive".

To me this silence felt like a terrible sacrilege. Every year that passed, Lucy, your birthday was spent with Mum. Even then there were not many words. It was somehow indecent to bring the subject up too much. The thought that it was going to go on like this until we all died and that would be that, was becoming intolerable to me. The regime of denial was crippling us. No-one else would speak about you, but eventually I needed to, in order to know that you had existed as part of our family for twenty-one years.

Lucy's disappearance taught me that beyond all doubt there is no certainty that, when you say goodbye to someone, you will ever see them again, that life is always changing and there seems to be nothing "out there" that can bring a feeling of security. In my twenties this hauled me through a lot of anger and confusion which was misplaced and had negative consequences. I certainly did harm to others. None of my friends quite knew how to relate to me going through this experience. Now saying goodbye to people, on a daily basis, brings with it that edge of intensity that accompanies the reality of impermanence.

This is the endless loop of the ultimate burglary. You return from a night out to find that all of the contents of your house have gone. Your blood surges with impotent rage, you want to pace, pummel and scream. Your body is coiled with fear, fury and reckoning. You are treading water and running, mute and loquacious. You can't think straight and yet where you find yourself has a clarity that feels closer to the truth. A veil has been rent. The place where you can feel safe stinks of invasion. You feel repulsion and a need to be held. There is no logic, only an instinct that roars like a river in full flood.

Imagine that you have mislaid something (a purse, a book that you needed to read, your bag, a pen, your passport). Part of you becomes preoccupied with needing to find it. Your mind goes into a state of not being able to concentrate on anything other than "where was it last seen?" It wasn't even stolen, you just can't remember where you left it. You want it to materialise, be there again. When you find it you realise that you aren't going mad after all. Life makes sense again. At last you can breathe a sigh of relief.

We went crooked, deformed by the secret of a missing sister. How do you grow straight when you wait with your secret, wait to know? The first year of Not Knowing was full of crookedness. A void, avoidance, a void dance, hopping on one leg.

It is very difficult to find the words or an image to describe the pain and disorientation of one's sister simply disappearing without trace, for twenty years. It's a bit like trying to search for a body which is trapped somewhere beneath the frozen Arctic Ocean, as the freeze continues and the ice thickens and there is no sign of a thaw, no sign of a seal hole. The features of that world become distorted as the seasons pass and the ice builds up and you have to go inside to get warm if you want to survive and carry on. But you have to be ready for the thaw, for the rescue. Somewhere inside I became disconnected from the past and disabled by the future.

Part of me was stuck in the past. Part of me was terrified of us all dying and never knowing what had happened to her. There was never a chance to honour her life. Eventually, twenty years after her disappearance and shortly before her remains were found, our family all gathered together to plant a special tree in memory of Lucy. This is how my daughter Marigold described it when she was sixteen:

Although it seemed like a good idea to put Lucy to rest the atmosphere felt really uncomfortable. Something wasn't quite right, because everyone found it really difficult to talk about her. This made me realise how painful the situation was and how devastating it was for them not knowing what had happened to her, and perhaps, never knowing.

There were occasional moments of light in the darkness. Soon after Lucy disappeared, I had a dream – the one referred to in the prologue. In the dream, Lucy had returned and I asked her where she had been. She said "I've been sitting in a water meadow near Grantham." Then slowly, with a smile, she said:

If you sit very still you can hear the sun move.

"Our" dream, you speaking to me from the water meadow, stands firm and proud in my mind. It is rooted like a weather-beaten hawthorn tree, wiry in the wind.

The feeling that came with Lucy's words in the first dream was of everything being in place, at ease, belonging. The place of harmony (the Greek "harmos" means "joint"), is where everything joins up. This is another possibility for silence – the place of "shining silence" where to speak would be to interrupt the wonder and mystery. In this place forgiveness is spontaneous. As the Chinese sage Lao Tsu wrote: "Harmony is the basis of existence, benevolence is the keystone of virtue". Right at the beginning of this journey, in 1974, the words of the dream gave me an experience that gave Not Knowing another dimension. It lay beyond the extreme of the fear, somehow dissolving it. It fed an undercurrent of trust in life. Whenever it was remembered it felt calming. Whatever happened to Lucy (if she was dead or alive) it was somehow all right because of the water meadow dream. It was Lucy's last gift and ultimate challenge to me. It dissolved the fear surrounding the reality of death and the uncertainty of Not

Knowing into a place of mystery and a longing to be informed, unravelled and liberated by this "Not".

The family continued to carry our pain in a stubborn, stoical, self-centred way. Mark and Dave continued to think that you had been murdered, but kept silent about it. Mum managed to keep going by thinking that the more years that went by the more likely it was that you were all right. She said she never lost hope. She had dreams about you walking past her, without recognising her, as if you were suffering from amnesia. She said that whenever she dreamed about you, you couldn't stay for long. It was as if you had something more important to do. Dad was immersed in his second family and living in the North of England. Somehow we were all trying to get on with our lives, each carrying the Not Knowing.

The first person in the village to talk to me about it was Norman at Gretton Farm. He had always been a sort of father figure to us after our father left us when I was twelve and you were eight. There was a warmth that he offered in his "What are you up to now then?" which had a feeling of non-judgmental, genuine care. Over the years he had nodded, pulled up, lowered the window and chatted from Landrover, tractor or combine harvester. There was no particular expectation. There was an honesty in the drawl of his Gloucestershire accent that allowed me to trust him. He could be harsh with his own daughters but he always seemed to have time for us. On the farm we were simply allowed to get on with it without any feeling of being judged or kept in line. There were always people and animals around. It was as if Norman knew what was needed. It was as if he knew that the question of what had happened to you was crushing me, and that there was no-one to talk to about it. But what he said next was the shock that was needed to jolt me out of the impasse that was suffocating me. He said:

I always thought she ended up being buried where they were digging up trenches for the new gas mains, you know, up by Cheltenham Race Course.

It was the first time, in eighteen years, that anyone outside the family had verbalised their imagining that you had been murdered. No words came. He did me a big favour by continuing with his theory, down to earth.

Well, whoever did her in, dragged her into a car, killed her and dumped her body in the trenches they'd dug for the new gas mains. It wasn't far from the bus stop on the Evesham Road. I don't know why the police didn't look there.

He was blunt, graphic, stunning. The information shattered the conspiracy of frozen silence. The violence of the language was authentic and closer to the truth.

To use the word "murder" was a huge risk. It would shatter the distortion of the past eighteen years. But even if we never found out the truth, the most likely ending was no longer a burden that we had to carry in dignified silence. Everyone in the village would have their own theory, their own memories. Suddenly the tourniquet could be untwisted. My blood was finding another course. Now, daring to imagine that you had been killed was possible. It was still abstract and it was about using the word "murdered" to myself; it was a bit like using the word "divorced" when our parents split up.

The new scenario was rehearsed by naming it to myself and living with the emotions that were seething around the word. The verb in the past tense did not have the power to put the feelings in the past, because we had no proof that it had happened. There was no body to bury. The word was like a magnet, drawing the feelings into my body. Words aren't as clever as they think. It could not be in the past tense until it had come into the present tense. How could murder ever join up with your world? My throat aching like the thawing of flesh, I set off to find the words, to speak, to break one form of silence in hope of another.

> *Memories*
> *played backwards*
> *leaping upwards*
> *like rain drawn back*
> *into a cloudless sky*
> *which doesn't want it.*

Pounding round
on a protesting treadmill
thaw up, kiss, mingle, fall
alight again.
It creaks,
and is agonisingly slow
but I am slower.
Its solid churning
makes a stiff waterfall
but I can't feel it.
Each jerky turning
drips words
of which I hear
perhaps one in twenty.
Running on stiff legs.
Lucy Partington

During the long Not Knowing, I bore my children. During my pregnancy with Luke, my firstborn, I bought a length of fabric from Liberty's. It bore a pattern of a robin with a worm in its beak, surrounded by green briars on a beige background. I made it into a cover for a piece of foam, to line the cradle that had rocked and held our cousins Matthew, Jonny and Sara. I bought a cluster of sequinned Indian toys to hang as a mobile above Luke: a lion, a tiger, and a star. When a candle was lit on the shelf next to his nursery corner, the special gifts from afar glinted, a constellation of birth.

Luke was born at home in north London, at 27 Winchester Road on 26th May 1976. It was a long, twenty-eight hour labour, and the cord was around his neck, but he arrived safely and his breath joined the dawn chorus before the sound of traffic began. His father, Nigel, bravely kept vigil attending with great care. It was a hot summer and I loved taking him to Primrose Hill to watch the London dawn and listen to the birds in the willow trees. By that time you were buried, Lucy, in what horribly became known as "the nursery corner" of the basement of 25 Cromwell Street. You were the second of five young women to be buried there between November 1973 and April 1975.

When Marigold was born, at home, at 125a Camden Street on 29th March 1979, it was sunny in the morning and snowing in the afternoon. I couldn't decide where I wanted to give birth. The independent midwife was Dutch and simply meditated in the corner of the sitting room. My friend Sally, who was training to be a doctor, was concerned about the hygiene if I decided to give birth in the sitting room. She swabbed the bare floorboards at the edge of the blue carpet where Luke played with his cars along the border with its patterned tracks.

I descended to the toilet half way to the basement. It was a good position, leaning forward from the toilet seat towards the edge of the bath. I stayed there for what seemed like a long time, but felt no need to move. The contractions were getting stronger and, to Sally's relief, I nested in the front bedroom of the basement. They followed me downstairs and the doctor arrived. I got stuck, lying on my back. I needed to stand up and dance, moving my hips and belly so that my legs joined up again. The doctor cheered me on. Marigold came out of me with a steady, smooth pace, head followed by shoulders and arms, followed by torso and legs. No one gave me an internal examination. I had been left free to give birth with no interference. It was 10 p.m. and I had been in labour for eight hours. The Indian doctor said that my new daughter looked "like an old soul who had been here many times before". Nigel shared his time between looking after Luke and sitting upstairs reading a book.

By the time Marigold was born, Nigel and I were living apart, mostly because he had been violent towards me. I was put on the "at risk" list by the health visitor. I was now a single parent with two small children in a council flat. The domestic "normality" of the Wests' lives was a fatal disguise for their depravity.

Fragments of images flood back: drunks in Camden Town; queues for food and buses with two small children tugging and straying; the smell of exhaust seeping into the basement of 125a Camden Street where Marigold was born; wolves pacing in Regents Park; elephants and flamingos glimpsed through the fence; bands on Sundays near the neat mounds of tulips by the boating lake; the canal path from Camden Lock to

Regents Park; the Greek shop on the corner with baklavas and taramasalata; the Greek restaurants with unglazed earthenware jugs stoppered by half lemons where we sometimes went at lunchtime; the sound of the traffic grinding into second gear as it moved away towards Euston; the chestnut tree and the old pear tree in blossom, bringing the magic of candles and lacy bonnets to the square of back gardens, where the woman next door took her dog for a crap each day, shovelling the shit into a plastic bag.

On his nightly visit out to the park, the Great Dane from the flat above us scratched the lino in the shared hall. The first night I moved in I thought it was rats. Brenda and Alan, the people upstairs, came down when I baked bread because of the smell of it. Their children were mesmerised by the candles and the real fire. Watching me caning and rushing chair seats, they began to make models in the evenings instead of watching the television that boomed through the ceiling day and night. Brenda and I were pregnant at the same time. Once, I got fed up with the dog shit in our bit of the garden and dumped it on her path. She hammered on my door shouting "fucking bitch". But the day after Marigold was born the family came down with pink congratulations cards, a yellow soft toy elephant and a second-hand pram.

In 1979, just six years after you vanished, I left Camden Town with my children. Did they absorb some of my unresolved pain? Often, when I watched them playing on the mountain, the freshness of their response soothed and inspired me. We retreated to an isolated *hafod* (summer farmhouse) called Gwartew, on a mountaintop in Mid-Wales, near a place called Staylittle (the Welsh is Penffordd Las which means "at the top of the green road").

On the surface, my life might seem to be untainted by the Not Knowing. But I was in exile, waiting to know – in the wind and the bareness of it all, with the ash keys brown and rattling in the gale, refusing to snap away from the twigs that bowed. In the distance, across the valley full of sheep, are the bare curves of Pumlumon (five peaks). On still days I loved sitting at the end of the garden, my back leaning against the rough scales of one of the three sentinel Scots pine trees. Here we could gaze at the place where the sun sets, the clouds form, the rain sweeps across. Here we could listen to the trill of the curlews marking the return of spring. Their song bubbles up like a kettle coming to the boil. Buzzards wheel and glide down to perch, with their claws gripping a fence post or telegraph pole. Harebells of the clearest sky-blue, and purple and yellow heartsease grow wild in amongst the tussocks of grass. When Mr Griffiths (our Welsh farmer-landlord) was dipping the sheep in his farmyard below us they looked like seething maggots. From here, we looked across to the source of the River Severn (Afon Hafren), marked on the distant horizon by cairns that look like a pair of nipples. Here I kept vigil for you, while my children grew.

Ten years after you disappeared, on 17th October 1983, my youngest son Jack was born. The labour began as I walked by the young River Severn with Nick, my dear partner since 1980 and now, since 2007, my husband. We were watching my stepson Aaron shoot the rapids in his canoe. I had planned for another home birth but there was bright red blood in "the show", and I was rushed off to Aberystwyth hospital with a suspected *placenta praevia*. Fortunately the birth was monitored and natural. Nick sat next to me rustling his newspaper and holding my hand as the hours passed and the transition came.

Lucy's friend Beryl arrived to support me and witness the birth. I didn't sleep all night because, as with Luke and Marigold, it was as if the utter wonder and mystery of giving birth was again laid bare, with shocking intensity. These fresh, tender lives had somehow passed through the ring of bone, moving from water to air. Each time I gave birth, it was like arriving in a new room where it was possible to know a state of being that was beyond the body of birth and death, and yet deeply embodied.

A year later the floor of the basement in 25 Cromwell Street was concreted over by Fred West. Some of the Wests' children slept above your bones. The basement had a change of use: from torture chamber to children's bedroom. Stephen West, Fred's son, remembers water and sewage from the cracked drains rising up through the concrete floor. The children paddled round the room in a wooden box. Stephen is terrified that he will become like his father. He was refused a mortgage because of his name.

One theory about the flooded basement is that it may have been the annual Severn Bore raising the water level. Anecdotes about the bore seeped into our childhood. Lucy, I wonder if you ever went to watch it? I never saw it, but I remember someone telling me about a wave higher than a man, surging back towards its source. Whoever told me said that people living in cottages by the river near Deerhurst had to move their furniture upstairs before it swept past, every spring when the moon was full, flooding over the banks and swilling through their ground floor. Then, I didn't connect its movement with the power of the moon, hauling the tide up twenty feet at the estuary, forcing a wave to rush backwards against the flow because the shape of the banks left it nowhere else to go. Then, I couldn't connect the word "bore" with its Old Norse roots, *bara,* a wave. Lucy, I wonder if you came across the word *bara* when you were studying Old Norse? I didn't.

I wish we could share our experience of Old Norse literature now. I seem to have lost my primer, but yours stayed on the bookshelf in your bedroom at The Mill. I sometimes "borrow" your books. I have reclaimed those that I gave you. It feels strange to take a gift back, but it helps me to remember you. Somehow books keep us close; your pencilled comments in the margins; my inscriptions to you, such as "Happy Christmas 1967, Lucy" in *The Poetry of Yevgeny Yevtushenko.* My writing has smudged and printed itself in reverse on the inside cover. The letters look as if they are steaming. They are beginning to dissolve. I treasure the poems that you wrote and left for us. When Mum died in 2009, your books joined up with mine.

In 1994, Mum and David were gathering your poems together for private publication. They had begun to do this just before your bones were unearthed. I had also felt a deep urge to plant a tree in memory of you, even before we found out the truth. In a strange way we were preparing for the shock of the discovery of your bones, what Dad called the "Last Chapter that we had all been waiting for". When Mum had gathered your poems, we planted the tree for you. It was as if we were preparing to know.

Listening to stripes
And watching the patterns of lace
Changing and crossing,
I remember
Last year's leaves
Which now lie buried
In memory's damp mould,
But the fibres last
Like bones,
Clung with fragments of thoughts.
They rot, in the unseen
Layers of the mind,
To feed the curling springs,
Until they become
Forgotten lumps of brown
Which will never again
Flicker on the branches
Which lull on the wind.
Lucy Partington

Your words haul the tides within me. I can bulge backwards on a wave that is bigger than a man.

When he was six years old your nephew, Jack, wrote this poem when he lived on top of the mountain in Penfordd Las. We did not know yet, but it was a year after the Wests had killed their daughter Heather and buried her under their patio. Jack and Heather were born on the same day of the year.

bubbling dripping water
falling from the sky
splashing on the mountain
coming from the high
streams turn into
rivers, rivers go on and
on, fishes go in the
estuary in to the
bright blue sea.
Jack Salt

It is as if the rain from our mountain tried to reach your bones, tried to purify them, set them free. In a mysterious way, this also frees me.

One day I walked for five hours, tracing the infant River Severn up to its source. Leaving the forest behind I struggled across the boggy, mountain moor. It was an unusually still, warm day. I reached behind the horizon, close to the cairns. The landscape on the top of Pumlumon is studded with giant toadstools of peat islands; black squat stems and straggly caps of last year's heather twigs and roots. Some are taller than me. They are called peat hags. Sheep erode their stems and leave traces of fleece.

Fortunately, peat doesn't cling to boots or smell like mud. It doesn't rot and squeezes out, like a sponge. I had just managed to haul out one leg that had sunk in up to my calf, and find a firmer foothold, when I looked up and saw the posts. The larger post is about eight feet high and is carved with "Tarddiadd Afon Hafren". The English post stands behind like a younger sibling: "Source of the River Severn".

The mountain seems to be gashed open. Lying on my front on one bank of dry peat, I am gazing into a silent, seeping and simmering of peat, moss, water, sky and grass, disturbing in its atavistic, delta rhythm. Is there any sign of the birth of a river? It seems to be an inexplicable, pre-germinal, formless place. If I put a foot wrong, it could swallow me and pickle my flesh for centuries. The larks, the sheep, and the buzzards have gone silent.

This insidious power is edged with fear. It reminds me of the monster Grendel in the Anglo-Saxon poem *Beowulf*. A bubble rises, so slowly, with defiance, from the depth of the black pool edged by stagnant moss. Two more appear and then within the stillness sounds the song of a lark in the distance. Now, on the surface of the pool, where the bubbles vanished, there is the faint swirl of a current, a welling up.

Now the sun brightens. It traces a capillary of water, pushing aside the waterlogged spring grass. The trickle casts an imprint of forked lightning onto the greenness: Tarddiadd Afon Hafren, source of the River Severn. It finds its voice when it gathers momentum and meets bedrock, cascading into white foam between the reeds, carving the peat and stones with the curves and smoothness of bones.

Birthdays were celebrated on the rocky skyline by releasing balloons into the wind, watching them recede into the sunset. On hot days we would go to Staylittle Stores to buy an ice-cream. The two miles of mountain road, past the lake and the rusting Landrover by the garage, have seen feet, pushchairs, tricycles, scooters, bicycles, horse and cart, donkey and cart, sledges and old banger cars.

After Staylittle Stores we would go down to the River Clywedog ("heard from afar") a tributary of the River Severn, by the chapel where it is shallow and flows gently, just right for young children to wade around and paddle in. Near the far bank is a seam of clay. It gleams like platinum on the riverbed near the overhanging grass of the bank. We would plunge our hands to the bottom of the river, gouging out handfuls and squelching it through our fingers. Then we would find a flat stone and leave it to dry off until ready for moulding. We sat in the sun playing with the clay. Remembering our wonky coil pots or mud creatures, I smile. Sometimes the children would smear each other with the grey, soft, sticky clay and decorate their slimy skins with grasses, rushes, flower petals, their bodies daubed with the richness to hand. Once Luke said "Spring is a green storm".

In 1991 we moved off the mountain into a valley (Llawr y Glyn), two miles away and six hundred feet lower. Three years later we found out most of what had happened to you, and where your bones had been hidden. I was glad to be in the shelter of wooded glacial slopes, out of the winter storms. It was like being sheltered by our Gretton Hill again. I had been exposed to the elements, stripped back to the bones of myself, waiting to know where you were, while my children grew.

Lucy, those years of Not Knowing were haunted by your unresolved absence. Something intangible and fragmented hovered beside me, reluctant to move on; waiting, searching, expecting me to suspend my life. Sometimes it strayed away but always caught up again, breathless and insistent. It got in the way, distracting me. I made destructive, rash choices that were sometimes hurtful to others. It was difficult to trust life and relationships. My friends did try to understand, and offered love, but at first I pushed it away. There was numbness, denial, isolation and confusion. My life was full of demands and this was a convenient distraction from allowing time for reflection. But there was always this part of me that had paused, waiting to know. During those years my inner life oscillated between these two polarities. At one extreme, as the years of Not Knowing passed by, as my children grew closer to leaving home, there was an increasing anxiety that we would all die and never know what had happened to Lucy. This feeling worsened as time went by. My missing sister was also a missing daughter, a missing aunt, a missing niece, a missing friend. But close to this fear was the anchoring, mysterious peace of the water meadow dream.

Chapter 3

UNEARTHING

By 1994, after seven years of attending Newtown Quaker Meeting, it felt right to be received into Quaker membership. Five weeks later we found out what had happened to Lucy. My initial feeling was absolute helplessness and inadequacy for the task ahead. I glimpsed, with unusual clarity, a long process of facing, accepting and letting go of decades of unresolved pain, and the spiritual implications of my recent choice to become a Quaker, that there is "that of God in everyone".

When I first heard of Lucy's terrible death, after twenty years of Not Knowing, I felt that I could either sink (be pressed down, drown), or turn into it with an open heart and learn something profound about my humanity. There was the potential for a deep lesson that could be passed on to my children and there was the choice to transform this trauma into "something good". I didn't know how or what, but a prayer to be shown the way filled every cell in my body. All the meaning of life seemed stripped away. There was no safety in any of my defences, nowhere to run. However, in the bareness of this Not Knowing there was a love that was already working within me, connecting me with all that has ever been.

Here are a few jottings from a diary written at the time. The only words that came to me are mostly brief and factual, coming from a state of shock and a certain amount of denial.

Tuesday 1 March 1994
Phone call from Mum warning me that the Press are suggesting that the third unidentified body that has been dug up in the garden of 25 Cromwell Street might be Lucy. They have been hassling her about it. The police haven't been in touch. They haven't contacted the police.

Wednesday 2 March
Came across a paper at work and read about the three bodies. Date of unidentified body female in late twenties. That evening phoned Mum and said I felt we should contact the police.

Thursday 3 March
Contacted the police in Gloucester. They said that they were following a line of inquiry and that they were almost certain that it was not Lucy. Because it's Lucy's birthday tomorrow and because the press speculation and horror of it all is stirring up our pain and anxiety, I decide to go and spend the day with Mum.

Friday 4 March
Lucy's birthday. Radio news before I set off has put the dates back on the third body (now died any time after 1972, body in early 20's). Also mention that West lived in Bishop's Cleeve which is on the bus route to Gretton from Cheltenham is making me feel sure that this must be something to do with Lucy. Spent the day keeping busy but feeling a terrible sense of unease and dread.

Saturday 5 March
10.15 a.m phone call from the police saying that they would like to come over to talk to us. They have some "news" for us. That half hour of waiting for them to arrive was full of a terrible restlessness and anxiety – palpitations and nausea. The numbness and muteness of shock began to invade. Two youngish plain-clothes

policeman arrived. They introduce themselves as Brian Smith ("Smudger") and Russell Williams. I notice Brian's polished brown shoes and his red tie and the scar on Russell's face. There is a pause. Then Russell confirms our worst fears. Fred West has been talking to the police and has told them that there are more bodies in the basement and that one of them is called Lucy. They have begun to dig. It was a lovely sunny afternoon and I felt like going for a walk up Gretton Hill. However we went shopping in Cheltenham. Denial was setting in. Numerous messages on the answering machine on our return. The Pain Vultures sound as if it's unquestionable that we should call them back (TV and major tabloids). We don't. By now they know that three more bodies have been recovered and that two families in Gloucestershire have been informed. Talk to Dad, he will come by train on Monday. Phoned Nick to say what has happened and that I must stay longer. I hardly slept that night. A paralysing feeling of weight, fear and a pain in my heart. This is enormous. Shock brings you into the present like giving birth. All your energy goes into focussing on surviving. Some people die of it.

The parents of the "other student" who was one of the West victims, Therese Siegenthaler, died of grief before they knew what had happened to their beloved daughter.

Sunday 6 March
Decide to go to Gloucester police station. Spent two hours with John Bennett as he tried to explain the complexity of the case especially in relation to the competition with cheque-book journalists.

We carried on south to break the news to two of my children at their Quaker boarding school. There was a deep anxiety that they might find out by watching the news at 6.00 p.m. We had to get there before then. By the time we had arrived they had already found out by phoning their stepfather, Nick. It was hard to leave them there but we agreed that it would be the best solution for all of us. All of their words and gestures expressed concern for my wellbeing.

That night I lit a candle and prayed. I didn't watch the news. In that moment I knew that getting caught up in the media presentation of this unbearable, complex crime would not be helpful. This was the beginning of a choice to trust that there could be another way forward that was free from media representations and distortions.

Tuesday 8 March
Back in Wales. Went to have my hair cut. I wanted to have it shaved off as a gesture to the world that I was grieving, that something huge had happened and that I wasn't the same as I was before it happened. I am beginning to understand how ill-equipped we are as a society for coping with mourning. It would be helpful to bring back some external sign that someone is grieving – black clothing has lost its significance since the Goths' fashion. While my hair was being cut (very short but not shaved) the news about Cromwell Street came on in the background. My hairdresser asked me what I thought about the awful goings on in Gloucester. I gulped and said something inane, thinking to myself, "Does she really want to know?"

Friday 11 March
From the depth of suffering comes a release and purification. The reality of Lucy's death rather than the imaginings of twenty years brings a renewal of the preciousness of each moment of life. I must find the courage to go on and face the worst kind of death imaginable and somehow try to understand it.

Easter soon arrived and we went to St. Davids for a family holiday as normal. The weather was cold and wet; the caravan steamed up as the rain lashed and the wind buffeted. This Easter we painted blown eggs as we always did. I painted a seal with its nose pushing through the surf (I'd just seen one near the beach) and a starfish sun. We walked to the cathedral for the family service to the sound of bells and seagulls.

On that holiday, my daughter Marigold decided to write a speech for the Annual Dymond Speech Competition at Sidcot (her Quaker school) about her experience of you, her aunt who disappeared. I first told her about you when she was four years old, ten years after you vanished. You would have been a brilliant aunt. You were so patient, imaginative and firm with younger children. Beryl, from Gretton Farm, remembers you encouraging her to read in a household of no books (though they did have the first eleven-inch television set in the village), and teaching her to play the recorder.

My second dream arrived soon after this holiday. I had just returned Luke and Marigold to Sidcot School and was breaking the journey home overnight in Bristol.

This dream gave me a bearing, charting my healing. It seemed to be bedded in my bones like the landscape of our childhood. Here it is in the words from my diary.

St. Pauls, Bristol, April 1994:
Sitting in Guy's garden with warming sun, daffodils, wallflowers and iris blades – a wren.

I had a very strong dream last night. Sitting in a room with lots of people. One person smoking and asking me insensitive questions about Lucy. So I got up and ran away onto a wooded hill top, wondering who to go and see. It felt good to be free outside.

I went into a house in which was Maria. The pathologist was there and I asked what were Lucy's "remains". He gaily said, "Look in that sack over there." There was a pink plastic sack. I pulled out some bones which were all covered in numbers like an anatomical chart. Next thing I knew, they were all assembled into a complete skeleton, which I embraced, the skull resting on my shoulder, then she started to talk to me. It felt very natural and I wanted to hold her for ever.

When I recollect this dream it gives the sensation of Lucy's physical being, the skeleton reclothed with her flesh, her shape that I remember. Awaking from this dream I felt an urgent need to know where Lucy's bones were. Until this dream it hadn't felt real. All those boxes covered in black cloth being carried out of 25 Cromwell Street were nothing to do with Lucy. They were to do with the world's media and "the public interest".

This dream initiated and symbolised the next step in the journey, the search for truth (factual, contextual and ultimate). It required honouring. We had all endured so many years of not knowing what had become of Lucy. A partial, premature and dangerous closing of our wound had been happening, because life can't be put on hold for twenty years.

Hold – perhaps now I can hold her forever? Dear Lucy, your spirit is now in peace, the remains of your body have survived so that we can know your physical ending twenty years ago. We will bury them in a place of beauty away from the cellar of brutality where you must have suffered unbearably. Even though it is painful for us now, we needed to know and will embrace you forever, healing all our wounds, learning how to live with love in a world of violence. *Agnus Dei*.

The legal process that we were trapped in moved slowly and beyond our control. It was time to respond to the dream, to rescue and protect, in some way, what remained of Lucy. Arrangements were made to go to Cardiff with two close friends. We went in the spirit of love with a need to make the experience more real and personal. We had waited twenty years to know where Lucy was and we still couldn't have a funeral. The investigation team at Gloucester kindly made the practical arrangements.

I would like to thank the dear man, the mortician, who allowed us to go beyond merely sitting in a chapel of rest next to a full-sized coffin covered with a purple cloth, fringed with gold tassels. I will never forget the look of understanding that came into his eyes when I emphasised that I wanted to place some special objects in with Lucy's bones. I know that some people might not understand my need to do this, but I have been pleasantly surprised by the number of people who did. It was a chance to love and cherish what was left of her. It was a chance to act, in a situation that was still out of our hands. It was a chance to reclaim her from her murderers and the hugely disrespectful, wretched hole in the cellar of 25 Cromwell Street.

The mortician began to unscrew the lid of the coffin to reveal two cardboard boxes. The larger of the two was exactly like the boxes in which I store my A4 files: a pale-grey DIY archive system, about 12" deep, 15" wide and 20" long. I felt a moment of panic. I pointed to the smaller of the two boxes, which was plain brown with a hinged lid, and asked: "Is her skull in there?" As he nodded and began to lift the lid, I was filled with the knowledge of what to do. A feeling of strength came over me.

As we drew nearer, I gasped at the beauty of her skull. It was like burnished gold and it was part of Lucy that had survived to tell the tale. I was full of the joy of finding something that had been a part of Lucy after all these years. Not a glimmer of fear, not a morbid thought entered the experience. I lifted her skull with great care and tenderness. My lips kissed the bone of her brow. I marvelled at the sense of recognition in its curves and proportion. I wrapped it, as I have wrapped my babies, in her soft brown blanket, her snuggler. I pressed her to my heart. Before I placed her skull back, I laid a branch of heather entwined with sheep's wool from the top of Pumlumon in the bottom of the box. I visualised the space and beauty of that wild mountain top on a summer's day: the brown peat, the sheep, the warm wind, the distant range of receding mountains, close to the sky. A place Lucy would have loved; a place that feels close to our Welsh roots; a place of freedom. I offered it with so much love.

Beryl, Lucy's childhood friend from Gretton Farm, placed Chocka (a much loved, very worn soft toy lion stuffed with straw) and One-eyed Bunny dressed in his smart velvet trousers, to sit either side of her wrapped skull, tucking a posy of primroses under Bunny's arm. These toys had been involved in endless games with us all as we grew up. Now they had the important job of guarding what was left of Lucy until we could have her back for the funeral.

I placed the egg that I had painted at Easter into one of the curved hip sockets in the ring of the pelvic bone. It was just like an egg-cup.

The mortician stood throughout this ceremony holding the lid of the larger box, nodding with approval. At one point he said "I wish more people could be doing this." When we had finally finished, he screwed down the lid of the coffin. We asked for some time to ourselves, and stood in silence holding hands. It was as if every member of my family was gathered there too, and eventually as if every woman who had suffered a violent death was also blessed in some way. This was another dimension, as if time had been transcended. We were united again at the "still point of the turning world". Something had been shifted. A step towards peace had been made.

Sometimes I return to the image of her skull as a way to release my grief. The orifices of the eye sockets remind me of the delicacy of her eyes that are no longer here, and never will be. They are empty holes, graves, the difference between being alive and being dead. The passing of time is reflected in the bones. The wonder at the durability of their substance and the beauty of their form increases my own sense of being alive. They remind me of my mortality and of my physical structure. I feel deeply grateful for that unique, very intimate experience, an opportunity to pay tribute to Lucy in my own way, to begin to say goodbye, for real.

By June the "remains" had still not been released for burial, so the careful plans for the funeral were put on hold. We decided to go ahead with our memorial gathering to celebrate Lucy's life. On a hot afternoon in July, 130 people gathered together at the Friends Meeting House in Cheltenham. My mother wrote:

Members of our family, childhood friends, school friends, university friends and teachers spoke eloquently and beautifully about their memories of Lucy, touching on every facet of her complex character. She lived again for us and we all came away feeling truly uplifted.

My daughter Marigold read an extract from her speech for the school competition. We all cried. These are some of her words:

There was one photograph of four children sitting on a pony. I didn't recognise one of them so I asked my mother who it was. She said it was her sister but she had disappeared when she was twenty-one. At the time I think I was too young to grasp the idea of her sister just "disappearing". But I remember feeling really confused when I looked at Mum because she was crying and I couldn't understand why.

When we used to visit our grandparents in Gloucestershire I always slept in "Lucy's room", which still remains similar to when she was last there. The house is an old converted cider mill and her bedroom is a small room where the apples were stored. When Lucy disappeared she was in her final year at Exeter University studying English, so the room is still lined with many of her books. When I slept in Lucy's room I always wondered if she would ever come back and what had happened to her.

I created this image of her returning. The whole family would be sitting eating lunch and I would look up to see Lucy walk across the lawn carrying loads of bags and run into the room where everyone was looking shocked.

Then Marigold quoted from the Quaker Peace Testimony:

All the darkness in the world cannot
put out the light of one candle.

A friend of mine who also became one of Lucy's friends rose to speak:

She was like a flame and implacably true. There was no place in her life for convenient compromise. I think we should see her life as a life completed, short though it was, not as a life disrupted and cut off too soon. She had, in her way, reached a culminating point where her early life was complete, leaving her ready for something quite new. The gifts she brought with her and which she gave to us, as well as her example, will stay with us, and no one who knew her will ever forget her nor remain untouched by her.

Elizabeth Webster who ran the Arts Centre in Cheltenham spoke of Lucy's imaginative contributions to this project. She concluded with this memory:

And then she came to see me when she was at Exeter, just before the last year, and I said to her, "Now that you are grown up what are you going to do?" and she said, "I don't mind what I do as long as I do it absolutely to the hilt." And then I said, "Yes that's fine, but where are you going?" and she thought awfully hard, then she said, "Towards the light... Towards the light."

Even in October 1994, Frederick West's solicitor insisted on keeping the "remains" as his "exhibits" despite the fact that they had been well documented by the police. The coroner wrote to him threatening to seek a judicial review of the situation.

Then, in December, the coroner wrote to my parents:

I have reluctantly to write to tell you and all other relatives and next of kin of the victims concerned in the Frederick West enquiry, to say that despite repeated attempts to reach agreement for the release of the remains, I have so far been unsuccessful...

Unfortunately I shall have to leave the matter over the Christmas period in view of the contentions put forward by those acting for Mr. West but you may rest assured that I will reconsider the position early in the New Year and may well take further advice as to whether, notwithstanding the lack of agreement, in view of my duty to all the relatives and indeed, of course, to the public at large, grounds may exist for me to release the remains irrespective of the wishes of those defending Mr. West.

Twenty days later Frederick West solved this problem by hanging himself. Later, during my restorative justice work in prisons, second-hand information that was buried in the minds of those who had worked with him emerged. It was shocking but more real than tabloid headlines. One prisoner claimed to have been on the wing in Winston Green prison when Fred died and suggested that he was murdered by the prison guards because they heard a lot of "shouting and banging". Later I was told, by the man who had to actually cut him down, that Fred West had smuggled the shirts that he was sewing buttons onto, as a work activity, back to his cell, and tied them together as a ligature. The banging was because his body was immediately in front of the door.

It was on our return from a New Year's Eve party with our next door neighbours that we learnt about Fred West's suicide. Our son Luke was leaning against the Rayburn in the kitchen after an evening at home because he hadn't been feeling well. He said, "The police phoned to say that Fred West is dead. He committed suicide." It felt wrong to me that he had been informed about this shocking news because we weren't there to take the phone call. Luke was eighteen at the time.

I never felt cheated by Fred West's suicide although many people thought that I should. Through my later encounters with people who had worked with him, he gradually became more real and human. Before he died I had thought that I might want to meet him about ten years later (I'm not sure why that length of time came to mind). The response was complex and changed with time.

Anne-Marie West told me that she was missing her father, because "at least he used to talk to me". She used to say to me, "People don't realise, Marian, I've lost too." (Yes: her father, her mother, her sister, her half-sister, her childhood.)

Rosemary West was on remand in Pucklechurch Prison. She was very angry when she was told about her husband's suicide. The police had to change the focus of their enquiry.

Rosemary West pleaded not guilty to the multiple charges of rape and murder brought against her. So, before the police could proceed with the trial before a jury, they had a preliminary examination of the evidence, called a committal hearing, before magistrates, to decide whether there was a sufficiently strong case against her to put her on trial before a jury. This took place in Dursley, near Gloucester, in February 1995.

Carol, who has been my mother's friend since they were eight years old, attended it with me. It was very comforting to be able to share this torturous experience. We both felt the need to find out as much as we could about the reality of Lucy's death before it became public knowledge. During my attendance at the trial we were truly supported by the investigation team, in a way that went beyond the job description. My only complaint was the dinners (but not the puddings).

It was almost impossible to match the figure of Rosemary West, sitting in the dock, with the endless graphic details of sexual depravities and brutality that were read out hour after hour for five days by the barrister. He spoke with an impeccable Queen's English accent and no emotion. The rigid structure of the court proceedings had the effect of anaesthetising the impact of the grotesque details of the case.

On hearing Rosemary West's voice on the tape-recorded police interviews about her relationship with her daughter, Heather, it became possible to have some insight into her mind. It was as if her deviant ignorance were rooted in an environment where fear and abuse were the main components. Her most common epithet, "bloody", was predictable but disturbingly accurate in the context of her world. To her, education was a "bloody load of rubbish".

Lucy, when you were abducted, Fred and Rosemary's first daughter Heather was three years old. Rosemary seemed to expect her to be "normal" in her teens in spite of the fact that she was being sexually abused by both parents. Rosemary said that Heather had to leave because she had lesbian tendencies (her uncle had put his hand on her knee and she pushed him away; she didn't have a boyfriend) and therefore she might be a bad influence on the younger children. By this time we had heard endless graphic details about Rosemary's sexual violence towards her own and other people's children.

Hearing that recording of Rosemary's voice, I was deeply shocked by her ability to lie so crudely and blatantly about Heather's "leaving home". At the moment in which Rosemary's story was being recorded in the police station, the police were digging up the patio at Cromwell Street where Heather was buried. Rosemary West was saying that Heather phoned them up sometimes, but she was often "bloody drunk". Lucy, did you realise that Rosemary was almost two years younger than you were and that she lived in Bishops Cleeve as a child? When I went to the dance at Bishops Cleeve Secondary School, Rosemary was living somewhere just around the corner.

And yet she managed to keep up appearances. About her children she said, "I kept them clean, fit, walked them to school, they never wanted for nothing." Heather "gave us a load of hassle when she grew up – they just do what they likes, when she left school she just sat in the chair"; "[it was] almost as if she didn't want to know me any more"; "once a child does cut you off there is not a lot you can do". Rosemary's extreme frustration about Heather emerged in her saying, "You can take a horse to water but you can't make him drink."

A picture began to emerge of the power struggle which led to the death of her stepdaughter Charmaine and her first daughter Heather; of the need to have absolute control and cause pain and ultimately death that was acted out in the night life at 25 Cromwell Street; of the involuntary, violent rage of impotence and ignorance that led to such terrible cruelty; of the impoverishment of a soul that knew no other way to live. Her behaviour was bestial and brutal in its attempt to make her victims experience a feeling of extreme pain, humiliation and terror (all of which, one can presume, she was made to feel in some way during her own childhood).

There was one little glimmer of insight into Rosemary West's imagination that both touched my heart and disturbed me. It was the only reference to beauty during a week full of endless statements of explicit, crude sexual detail that were expanded upon in the trial. It was her attempt to lure Alison Chambers to come and live in Cromwell Street by promising her a life in the country at the weekends on "their farm" where she would be able "to ride horses and WRITE POETRY".

The image conjured up Lucy's world (Lucy spent a lot of her childhood involved in both activities). Sweat pricked my armpits. Had Lucy had a chance to speak to them? Had they read about her life in the media shortly after they killed her, when we were desperately searching for her? Or was it simply just one little moment when the world of the Wests brushed against Lucy's world? That detail was used to lure another victim to their lair. There was something about the use of the word "poetry" that leapt out of the general mire of blasphemy and made my stomach churn. Another such moment was when we heard that their last child was called Lucyanna.

> Lucy, when I kissed your skull,
> The dome of the sky took root in my heart,
> You have not died.
> We shine, burnished by grace.

Rosemary had been abducted from a bus stop and raped when she was fifteen years old, before she met Frederick West when she was sixteen. That was only four years before they abducted you, Lucy, from the bus stop near Pitville Park. Rosemary's body already knew both incest and rape. Could she, who was described as "just a child herself" when she met Fred, find a truth beneath all her inveterate pain? Could she find some words that are true? Lucy, did you know her name?

It was unexpected to hear from people who had actually met Rosemary West and worked with her, but later I learnt that her father and Fred West and his brother John groomed and abused Rosemary as a fifteen year old girl. Fred's sexual depravity (egotistical needs, psychopathic needs?) became increasingly violent. Rosemary lived in a state of constant fear for her life and in awe of Fred's power. She has fully admitted to her involvement in the abduction of "the victims" and some of the sexual violence, but maintains her position of being innocent of their deaths. For her they were a temporary escape from the terrible violence being perpetrated upon her. Is it possible to believe that her fear kept her ignorant of the final demise of the "victims", who apparently died because of the prolonged violence of the sexual torture and abuse? Death was a side-effect rather than the original aim of the exercise. It terrifies me to think of this. It is beyond my comprehension. Here I cannot dwell.

> *Is there truly "that of God in everyone"?*
> *Lucy, when I kissed your skull*
> *The dome of the sky took root in my heart.*

She left Fred and his brother John to have "their evil way" and returned to the domestic demands of the household. I had guessed at her ability to keep up a front. The "facts of the case" and the way that they were manipulated during the trial were only small aspects of the truth that was sought. More than this, there was a need for understanding of the intricate context of human relationships within our society. Ultimately, there is a need for meaning, resolution and healing. The later trial and the sentence did not answer my need to know the truth of what happened to Lucy. Human justice is mostly focussed upon retribution, causing more pain. Our human potential is not enlarged by this punitive process. Healing is imprisoned.

Chapter 4

RE-EARTHING

Nine months after our first visit to Cardiff, and a week after the committal proceedings for Rosemary West, Beryl and I returned to Cardiff. Frederick West's death meant that at last we were free to proceed with the funeral. We had arranged to meet the undertaker from Exeter. She had been a student at Exeter University and was entirely supportive of any way that we chose to deal with this momentous occasion, charged as it was with a huge need to express our love and our grief. Nick, then my partner, now my husband, had made a simple box for Lucy's bones. It looked like a medieval chest and was made from seasoned Welsh oak (kindly donated by another friend). The handles were made of thick rope. Patrick, my woodcarver boyfriend at the time of Lucy's disappearance, who by then lived in Houston Texas, sent a plaque of antique oak into which he had carved Lucy's name and dates:

LUCY KATHERINE PARTINGTON 1952–73

Nick had carefully mounted this with pegs on to the end of the box. This end became the "head end" for the purpose of carrying the coffin in and out of the church.

This time we had to go to the mortuary. The porter took a while to understand why we were there. He had to lock up at 4.00 p.m. It was already 2.45 p.m. The file box with its black, felt-tipped marking "JR5 Body 6" and in red felt-tip "Lucy Partington" awaited us on a trolley in the hall. This was my sister's last bureaucratic resting place. I had to reassure the porter that we had already seen the bones.

This society suffers badly from a fear of the reality of death. In Tibet human thigh bones are lovingly made into instruments of great ceremonial importance. The sound of breath blowing through bone cuts through to the quick.

Eventually the porter remembered that there was a chapel of rest next to the hall-way. We were shown in, with the reminder that we had to be out by 4.00 p.m. The room had obviously been out of use for years. The mantelpiece was shrouded with dust. Inside the box, the blown egg that had been lovingly painted at Easter, with an image of a seal poking its nose out of the sea and a star-fish sun, and placed carefully in the cup of the pelvis socket during our previous ritual, had been broken.

It was time for the final reordering of the bones. We placed sawdust in the bottom of the box and then a length of tweed that I had bought the previous autumn while exploring the wilderness of the Isle of Harris. We placed the skull at one end of the box Nick had so lovingly made from Welsh oak, the pelvis at the other. Between these we laid the arm and leg bones. The vertebrae were threaded on a piece of rubber. We unthreaded them and laid them in order with the sacrum and coccyx next to the pelvis. The scapula, collarbone and ribs were arranged as symmetrically as possible in relation to the skull and the vertebrae. Handfuls of wrist and finger and toe bones and the patella were placed under the pelvis. The heel bone was puzzling because it was quite small and looked as if it needed a socket with its ball-like end.

After organising the bones as much as possible we moved on to the gifts. First, a copy of the book of Lucy's poems that my mother and stepfather had painstakingly collected together and published for family and friends was tucked behind Lucy's skull – but only after we had read a few of the funny poems aloud, particularly one about Felix, our pony. My father had sent a rosary blessed by the Pope. My younger son had sent his crucifix, that he had bought from a nun during a holiday in France. My elder son's offering was a piece of blue, shiny enamel work he had made. My daughter gave an intricate drawing of a Celtic knot. Nick gave a small jar of honey from our bees. Behind the pelvis I tucked a picture of the Dalai Lama. Chocka and Bunny and the soft brown blanket went in next. Finally Beryl laid one of her most beautiful weavings (a rich maroon Ikat scarf) over our treasure and we screwed down the lid. We carried the box out to the undertaker's car and she drove off to Exeter.

On 16th February 1995, 17 days short of a year since we had found out what had become of Lucy, approximately 21 years and 7 weeks after her death, we could have the funeral. The requiem mass, hosted by the Catholic Chaplaincy at Exeter University, and celebrated by Lucy's priest, was full of the beauty and love that she deserved. Many of the friends and relatives who had attended the memorial gathering the previous July were there, also various friends who had been unable to go to that gathering. Three of the investigation team sped down the M5 to be with us.

A massive exercise in security and silence, respected by everyone within the university, successfully ensured that the Press were unaware of the ceremony: no Pain Vultures were present. It was particularly moving to see and hear the choir singing and the musicians playing. They were all present-day students to whom Lucy was a sad but rich legend. At the end of a requiem mass, the antiphon *In Paradisum* is sung:

> *May the angels lead you into paradise:*
> *may the martyrs receive you at your coming,*
> *and lead you into the holy city, Jerusalem.*

The following day our family and a few close friends met at a tiny medieval church near our home. We were about to perform the penultimate ceremony. There had been much discussion within the family about whether to cremate or bury Lucy's bones. My youngest son voiced what became the general consensus: "Lucy has been buried in a horrible way for twenty years, I think we should bury her in a nice way now." It was clear to me that she should be laid in consecrated ground, that we should have a grave and that her bones should be left in peace rather than being ground up, which is what would have happened to them if she had been cremated and just scattered. It seems that it was the right decision because the grave has indeed become a place where we can go to remember and pay tribute to her, and grieve. Having lost her for so long there is some comfort in having finally laid her to rest and in knowing where her bones are buried.

Fortunately there was room for a grave in the churchyard of a place that was very special to Lucy. It was a place that she used as a retreat when she wanted some time to herself when she was younger. More recently she had been writing a thesis on the medieval wall paintings that continue to decorate the interior. The images that oppose each other on the two main walls of the nave are strangely disturbing: one of them contains echoes of the violence surrounding her death and in the other there is a clear reminder of the strength of her faith.

The violent image is of a hunting scene. The hunter brings up the rear of the chase. The hare is cornered and the hounds are about to pounce. Lucy's unfinished thesis observes that there are various interpretations for this, and raises a question as to what the hare represents. My initial reaction was to see the hare as a vulnerable soul about to be pounced upon by hounds.

On the opposite wall stands a figure of St Christopher, at least eight feet tall, wading through the sea with the Christ Child on his shoulder and a staff in his hand. The patron saint of travellers, he is often painted near church entrances. He chose to serve God humbly by acting as a "ferry on foot", carrying travellers across the river.

After a brief service Lucy's box was carried out into the cold wind by my father, my brothers and me. It had rained almost every day for three months and just at that moment a shaft of sunlight poured down from behind a cloud. The three priests (Lucy's priest, the local vicar and Lucy's godfather) stood in a line in their billowing white robes. Lucy's priest blessed the grave. The sun shone on and we lowered the box into the earth. As we all drew near to gaze into the grave a bantam cockerel appeared from nowhere, nonchalantly scratching and pecking. During our childhood we kept bantams. Lucy used to try to paint them sometimes. There was something deeply reassuring about this moment, as if we had done all that we could to express our love for Lucy and there was a sort of reply going on – a real blessing. The undertaker commented later that she had never experienced the length and quality of the silence that held us all in that moment.

An image of my mother is clear in my memory. She stood by Lucy's open grave, small and frail in her black coat, with her white hair short and stiff like a skull cap. Her hands were holding a small posy of flowers from her garden, picked earlier in the morning. She moved towards the grave as if she were not quite Lucy's mother and it were not quite happening, this moment that we had all dreaded and longed for: the laying Lucy to rest after twenty-one years of not knowing where she was or what had happened to her.

Eight months later, Rosemary West's full trial before a jury was about to begin. The profoundly shocking details of life in 25 Cromwell Street were in the public domain. The possibility that children might watch the horrors on the news or read them in the papers caused me great anxiety and concern. In my imagination a dream vision arose: there could be a national campaign to hang poems in trees in memory of all victims of violence. In this way an opportunity for people to make a positive gesture in the midst of the onslaught of the West trial could be created, so that the focus of public attention could be on the tragedy of the deaths of those who died, rather than on the murderers and their profound sickness.

The idea for the poetry campaign came from one of Lucy's favourite poems by Yevtushenko called *I Hung a Poem on a Branch*.[7] Here is an extract:

if we have trouble on the way,
   we'll remember
      that somewhere,

           bathed in light,

  a tree
    is waving
      a poem
   and smiling we'll say:
      "We have to go on."

When most of us were kissing pictures of the Beatles, Lucy was kissing a picture of Yevtushenko. The book of his poems was my gift to her for Christmas 1967. She was studying Russian 'O' level at the time.

Unfortunately, my time and energy did not extend into putting my campaign into practice, although many trees were hung with poems after 1996, in response to the Guardian essay *Salvaging the Sacred*. At that time, though, it was exciting and inspiring to discover Tibetan prayer flags. They hang like rows of bunting, bright-coloured rectangles of cloth printed with spiritual blessings. In an ancient ritual, they are renewed each year to signify hope, transformation and the spreading of compassion. As the year progresses, the wind disperses the energy of the words, which carry the power to pacify and heal everything they touch. A row now charts the wind outside my kitchen window. Filling and emptying, they flap and fray, tracing the invisible.

For the first few weeks of the trial it was possible to ride the storm by relying upon D.C. Russell Williams (our liaison officer from the investigation team) for information. My focus was determinedly upon my family and my work, so I chose not to attend the trial in person. Over the last two years Russell had become "Russ" and kept us informed of the progress of the case. He was there to answer any questions that we had. He always gave us advance warnings of media releases before they hit the headlines. Throughout the trial he phoned with regular reports from Winchester, so it was unnecessary to read the distortions in the Press. When they did leak through we could ask for clarification.

Then the Fred West tapes were played. Someone phoned to commiserate with me about a report by *The Times* which printed the obscene words verbatim. *The Times* even added to the degradation by printing the story under a tabloid subheading. The media reporting could no longer be avoided. At my request Russ provided me with a large bundle of newspapers. Fred West said that Lucy was "just a girl I was knocking off". He claimed that after three months of what was "purely sex, end of story" she had "come the loving racket and wanted to live with me", making out he was doing her a big favour and that it all went wrong because she wanted more than he did. He said "I grabbed her by the throat and then I drove back to Gloucester. I brought the van up over the pavement, then I knocked the engine and lights out and let him cruise down to the back." In his description, Lucy and the van were both subjected to a "knocking" of one sort or another.

He didn't seem to discriminate between the objects of his brutality. He lumped all his victims into the same category, just bodies that were soon deprived of any individual identity, as their voices were muted and their features were smothered under the masking tape gags that lasted longer than the flesh they were glued to. During his garbled confessions we could see his total lack of connection with reality, in his attempts to justify the killings as if somehow they weren't really all that much to do with him, as if they were happening in spite of him, like some snuff movie going on in the background. The fantasies were as disarticulated as the bodies by the time he had finished with them. He said about one of the victims "I strangled her or held my hands round her neck." Struggling to understand this warped logic, I wondered if his repetitive, sadistic behaviour was some sort of attempt to get in touch with a feeling of being alive.

The thought that even one person might have believed his words was unbearable.

We had been warned that the prosecution had chosen this tape partly because it was easy to prove that Fred's explanation about why he had to kill Lucy was insane fantasy. My mother's statement made this clear, accounting for the time that Lucy was supposed to have been involved with him. This could also be backed up by Exeter University and by the priest who was preparing her for entering the Catholic Church in November 1973.

In fact, it was the defence who used the tape, because it had a statement about West being the only person involved in the murders. So for three days it hung in the air, unchallenged. This was a time of great agitation. Brian Leveson Q.C., barrister for the Crown Prosecution, assured my father that he would make it very clear in his rebuttal that the tape was a cruel lie. However, the press obviously found it less important to print the truth. It wasn't sensational enough.

What was it that so incensed me concerning West's fantasies about Lucy and the way they were published? What he did to her was far worse. It was something to do with the crude level of language that was so far from Lucy's passionate love of the poetic. It brought out my rage at the inappropriateness of Lucy's death, which just did not seem fitting to her life. It made me aware of the vast gap I needed to cross in order to be able to comprehend and forgive.

It was as if anyone who heard or read West's words became a victim of his pornographic delusions; the print seeped into the air, as insidious as nerve gas. The words poured out by the skip-full, vile gabblings, an endless rubble of lies. They revealed the completely egotistical, brutish mentality of a human being who was utterly devoid of any sense of truth about himself or anyone else. Not only had he performed these monstrous murders but he had then distorted the truth about them into further pollutions, extending his cruel trademark. It was truly blasphemous.

There was no choice but to crusade. My next chance to protest was during Leveson's summing up, in which he focussed even more strongly on just how obscene the fantasy was in relation to Lucy's life. Even though the Press Association had been asked to brief the journalists covering the West case to pick up on that point and print it, no words appeared. The police suggested that we could make a statement after the trial if we still felt it was necessary. The subject was raised in a meeting with Leveson during the lunch hour at the judge's summing up in Winchester.

It was impossible not to fight for the sensibility of Lucy's whole being that is so clearly reflected in the carefully chosen words of her poems. Russ gently reminded me that we were dealing with murder, not Lucy's life. Fortunately, Leveson could understand my feelings, especially on hearing two of Lucy's poems. His last words to me were "I'm off to speak to the press about a subject that is dear to your heart." Apparently he briefed each journalist individually, and that evening the news on radio and television put the jury's task into a nutshell, using Lucy as a focus. They had to decide between Fred West's version and Lucy's mother's statement. Why would Fred West have felt it necessary to create his story about Lucy if it wasn't to protect someone else (i.e. Rose)?

On 19th March, a message was left on my answering machine:

Hello, Marian, it's Russ. Just to let you know that Rose West's leave for appeal has been turned down this afternoon, despite the fact that it was due to go on until the end of the week. As far as we're concerned, that's the end of the matter. If you want to give me a ring you can. Thanks very much...message ends.

This was an abrupt, confusing moment. Now we were alone after an intense involvement with the criminal investigation. It was the end of the matter as far as the criminal justice system was concerned, and in some ways the beginning of the matter for us.

I attended the judge's summing up at Winchester partly because it was the best opportunity to thank and hug Detective Superintendent John Bennett (the senior investigating officer), Detective Chief Inspector Terry Moore (acting as deputy senior) who used to travel on the same school bus as me, and dear Russ. "Good on you all" as we say in Gloucestershire. I felt a great need to express my gratitude to all those people who gave of their best during this deeply traumatic experience: family, friends and professionals, the jury and the witnesses.

Whilst there, I had a brief experience of unconditional compassion. Anne-Marie (Frederick West and Rena Costello's daughter, Rosemary West's step-daughter) was sitting behind me in the gallery, a few feet away. It was her gruelling evidence of continual sexual abuse by Fred and Rosemary West that was being dealt with during this session. I felt profoundly sad for her. As we stood up to leave, I found myself reaching out my hand towards hers and saying something inadequate but heartfelt. We both had tears in our eyes. She moved her hand towards mine and touched it lightly. I am not sure if she knew who I was.

Commitment to "good" seems vital to our survival. It is a journey that each one of us needs to take. It involves looking at the darker side of our human nature as well as the lighter side. Events like this hold a mirror up to our society.

Later I was to meet Abagayle, whose daughter, Catherine Blount, had been brutally murdered in California. After eight years of bitterness and hatred she had felt the need to contact her daughter's murderer. Their eventual meeting transformed her life. She gave me a phrase that I now have pinned to my door: "Forgiveness means giving up all hope of a better past."[8]

Confessing

Chapter 5

ENFOLDING THE DARK

This chapter is concerned with the importance of staying with darkness, in order to move through and beyond it. It has been the most difficult to write. It concerns itself with that which I wish had never happened, the bits that I would prefer to edit out, which stand in the way of growth and fulfilment, in the way of truth.

If I wish to move towards forgiveness, towards "giving up all hope of a better past", I must acknowledge that to fabricate a "better past" means manipulating one's story and basing one's sense of reality upon the delusion that whatever has happened didn't really happen (denial), and that something better could have happened. This fabrication becomes riddled with secrets and corrosive, afflictive emotions. It is an attempt to avoid the pain of whatever it is that we cannot face and accept about our past.

Confess (verb): con- (prefix): *together, together with, in combination or union, altogether, completely* + Fatere, fass: *to utter, declare, disclose, manifest, avow, acknowledge.*

Confess: *to declare or disclose (something which has kept or allowed to remain secret as being prejudicial or inconvenient to oneself) to acknowledge, own or admit (a crime, charge, fault, weakness).*

To confess is to begin to allow the frozen story of that which lies beneath the deluded "better past" to melt. The roots of the word suggest that this is a movement towards union and completion. It involves all those who have been hurt by you and those who have hurt you. It involves expressing and living through the confusion and pain of laying bare that which has been "prejudicial and inconvenient" to one's deluded identity and the "truth" of others affected by this disclosure.

To confess involves a need to speak out and be heard, so that whatever is compressing one's heart/mind, troubling one's spirit, can be received and witnessed. It is something about a need to move out of one's self-centred prison and trust that by sharing whatever it is that deadens one's being there can be a release and renewal. It is something about acknowledging and uttering forth that which corrupts and destroys our capacity to love and be loved. Whatever it is, however it comes about, it is an essential part of finding one's authentic voice, finding fresh words and being heard in the hope that one can "come clean".

How do we become liberated from that which we would prefer to edit out or deny? Where is the place to express this hidden, deluded aspect of ourselves, and to whom? The words "confession", "sin", "repentance", "forgiveness", "grace", "redemption" (let alone "God") are barnacled with centuries of religious connotations, misuse and abuse. Yet the secular mind is not free from a moral conscience, guilt, shame and a yearning to be free from these crippling emotions. The vocabulary of psychotherapy attempts to cover this territory. To whom do we confess? Is it necessary to be heard or is there a place within our right to privacy for choosing not to disclose our "prejudicial and inconvenient" secrets?

The boundaries between "private" and "public" have been deeply challenged by Lucy's identity as a "West victim". Decades of the Wests' sexual depravities and murders were buried in the garden and in the cellar of 25 Cromwell Street. Their secrets, their depravity, hovered in our lives too. Depravity (Latin pravitus, pravus): *crooked, perverted, corrupt.* Some of the Wests' secrets became public. Frederick West confessed a garbled truth, Rosemary West remains silent. Our family found itself in the midst of a high-profile crime, at the mercy of the Pain Vultures at a time when we needed privacy. For me it was vitally necessary to find and add my voice, as Lucy's sister.

In 1999 the Anglican priest Canon David Self invited me to contribute to his book on forgiveness[9] that he was writing during a three-month sabbatical from his work as a priest in the violent, drug-torn community of St. Pauls in Bristol. During a long interview (a confession?) I expressed the realisation that it seemed pretentious and hypocritical of me to think that I could forgive the Wests before I had actually faced up to the other people in my own life by whom I needed to be forgiven and whom I would like to forgive. I said:

In a way I am left with trying to stay true to what is actually happening and avoiding nothing. That's where the teaching seems to be.

He responded with this insight:

Acknowledging the darkness in the world led Marian to face the darkness in herself – the capacity for huge rage and murder that lies in the heart. If she had refused to take that step, the next would have been to deny her own darkness and project it onto others. The pain would have remained inside and might have led to all sorts of unacknowledged destructive behaviour, such as a life of bitterness or addiction.

He went on, with a message of hope, which sustains me.

[We need]... to realise that the mess we make in our own lives is precisely the place where God is the most creative... There has been so much atrocity in this past century, that without the quiet struggles of many people who enfold the dark creatively and grow with integrity, there would be little hope for us. There are more candles in the dark than we realise.

The question of how to find an inner strength that could somehow transcend the reality of human atrocity and enable me to trust life had become an urgent quest in the wake of Lucy's murder. Initially it was important to affirm the worth and beauty of her life, "that of God", but there was also the darkness of what had happened that needed to be faced without being overwhelmed by it. My forgiving of the Wests can only begin with facing my own rotting pile of mistakes and woundings. It is easier to see women as victims of male-perpetrated violence than to face the reality that women are also violent, towards other women, towards men and towards children; that women feel and express rage.

I have given birth to three dear children. But, between 1970 and 1985, I chose to terminate four pregnancies. It is with anxious shame that I acknowledge this. Two were before you died, Lucy. The third was in 1974, during the first year of your disappearance. Why did I do it? The first three pregnancies were conceived within loving, confused, immature relationships. The first two involved the same father, Pete, whom I had met at university in 1968.

I was using different forms of contraception. Firstly, there was the pill, which seemed to have frustrating side effects, including putting on weight and sexual apathy. I tried different kinds and became pregnant when I changed brands and had not been informed that extra contraception was needed for the first two weeks. At the time it seemed impossible to imagine a positive future for this first, embryonic child, both personally and within the larger context of the future of the world, or to connect with the pregnancy emotionally at all. Apart from swelling breasts there was no sensation of being pregnant. It did not feel real that there was a new life growing in my womb. At the time we felt that this was the right decision, although it was the most lonely, terrible choice to make. I remember the deep confusion, the pressure of time, the huge fear and the hostility of some of the NHS staff.

By the time of the second pregnancy, two years later, my relationship with Pete had become more unstable. I had not really processed the grief about the first abortion and was struggling with bleak depression, as well as with my English degree. We were using the cap, or rather trying to use it in a somewhat haphazard way; the contraceptive cream and the size of it involved more forethought than male condoms. Even though I had friends who had made the choice to terminate pregnancies, it remained a shameful subject that was not talked about.

The third pregnancy was mired in the aftermath of Lucy's disappearance, when I was finishing my English degree, addicted to falling in love and pushing away emotional intimacy. I had now moved onto the dreadful copper seven coil, which had to be removed because of heavy bleeding and pain and a terrible feeling of internal agitation. My boyfriend at the time, Patrick, who was much loved by our family, had returned briefly to America after seven years in exile. The amnesty for "draft dodgers" was announced soon after Lucy's disappearance. I had tried to escape from the pain of this disappearance and my boyfriend's temporary departure by plunging into an intense affair with Michael, a university lecturer. The mess was getting worse. I conceived in the midst of my final exams and did not know who the father of the child was. Patrick, with humbling generosity, offered to marry me and bring up the child, even if he wasn't the father. I was truly loved and truly forgiven and yet I made another negative choice.

The fourth and last abortion in 1985 was the most difficult, because by then I had given birth to three dear children, and gained an older stepson, my husband Nick and his first wife Cathy's child. This had taken me into a new relationship with life. Nick and I met in 1979 in mid-Wales. Our son Jack was born in 1983. Nick was very clear about not being able to support any more children, having four between us. He kept saying that we must put our energy into our children and not stretch ourselves even more. With great pain I chose to have a "conscious" abortion, with a local anaesthetic. I had never been offered that in the past and didn't know it was an option. It was in a private clinic this time. The "suction method" was applied and I tried to stay in touch with the reality of the process, trying to connect with the foetus, with desperate apology, prayer and terrible sorrow. I feel afraid of harsh judgement when people read these words. Nick chose to have a vasectomy after this, which made me realise just how much my sexual life had been dominated by a fear of pregnancy.

At times I have been overwhelmed by a feeling of terrible remorse and shame about the abortions. These feelings were intensified by the birth of my children. Whatever the consequences, known and unknown, to my life and the lives of others (the fathers, grandparents, grandchildren, siblings, aunts, uncles, nephews, nieces, cousins and the unborn children) this "editing out" seems almost impossible to expiate. It is not consoling, but true, that this has helped me to feel more compassionate towards those who have killed, legally or illegally.

In my mind, I reach out towards women who have died as a result of illegal abortions; women who have been unable to have children and wanted to; women who have suffered still-births and miscarriages, and women who give birth to children in the midst of poverty, war, rape, famine, epidemic disease, natural disasters and domestic violence.

Facing my own violence as a woman also led me to recognise my feelings of impotence and anger as a young adolescent caught up in the divorce between my parents. The violence was not physical, it was psychological.

When I was twelve, in 1960, I remember asking myself the question: "does sin grow out like bruised nails?" It was when Dad first left and I was blaming myself. The pain of knowing he was alive and not wanting to be with us any more was almost unbearable. He was the first missing person in my life. It felt as if he would be better dead rather than living somewhere else with someone else.

It is easier to hate than to love. Hatred freezes its objects in the place of delusion and death. My teenage years were rooted in this feeling of unspoken loss and the frustration within this enduring confusion of split loyalties. The stigma of coming from a "broken home" was real in the late 1950s. My solace was going for long rides on Gretton Hill, taking refuge in solitude and nature.

Whenever my anger came out I was accused by my mother of being "just like Roger" (my father): "If you can't think of anything nice to say don't say anything at all." I erupted into rebellion. The teenage culture was waiting for me. The first generation of consumers after the Second World War was being seduced by fashion. The Beatles and Biba (a cutting-edge fashion boutique in London), offered an external identity. My brother Dave formed a rock band called "The Disease", spurning our father's hope that he would continue with the local scouts. The era of cider, "Number 6" cigarettes, Lambrettas, Jimi Hendrix and the Blue Moon crept into the house along with the Sony record player and the early Beatles LPs.

Our home at The Mill became a haven for friends escaping strict parents. The liberal chaos seemed inviting, along with the home-made bread and lack of boundaries. Were we lucky to be free of our father's oppressive influence? It didn't feel quite safe somehow. But there were always regular, delicious meals, clean clothes and a polished house with a large garden. We were not encouraged to take responsibility for domestic chores. I remember my mother, in a rare moment of anger, accusing me of being "a fat lazy slob". I agreed with her but felt ignorant about how to change this feeling of stagnant selfishness.

I can still see Father crying over the steering wheel in the lane outside The Mill. He was returning us after an outing to the cinema: Cliff Richard's *Summer Holiday*. I had cried when the family drove off in their convertible car and Cliff sang, "We're all going on a summer holiday." I had also taken to blushing in history lessons every time the word divorce was mentioned: we were doing Henry VIII. Divorce was uncommon and almost taboo. Seeing my father crying over the steering wheel, I go back. Father asks me if he should come back; I say "I don't know." I am in fear of his coming back, fear of telling him I would rather he didn't come back. Mum has red-rimmed eyes. I can't stand the shouting when we are in bed upstairs.

He did come back, but not for long. He brought all his new furniture, including bunk beds, and put it in the Big Room. Mrs Brown, our cleaner of many years, complained that she couldn't clean the room properly. She kept polishing the concrete floors with Ronux and the electric polisher. The gravel in the concrete was like trapped beads beneath the brown patina. Father was sleeping downstairs on the bunk bed. Father was leaving again. Later we discovered that during his absence he had been having electric shock treatment for manic depression. He took a job in Pontypool with British Nylon Spinners. The winter was too cold for him to travel back to us. He met a midwife at a dance hall – his next wife, Tessa.

They moved to Abergavenny and we didn't see Dad for a year. He phoned to tell me that I had a half-brother, Paul. I felt as if I was going bad inside, like a pebble trapped beneath polished concrete. I was confused, lonely, angry, rebellious. I galloped around the forty-acre field down the Working Lane where we used to play the Famous Five. I beat my horse, Piper's Dream, with a stick, harder and harder and jagged her mouth with the reins. I tried screaming, masturbating, not talking, being "a fat, lazy slob". In 1966 my half-sister Julia was born.

Dad, I have thought about what it must have been like for you, when your mother committed suicide – my grandmother that I never met, whose name I carry, Marian, just as I named my eldest child Luke in memory of Lucy, and gave my daughter Marigold the second name of Lucy. Perhaps there was a passing on of unresolved pain in some way, burdens to be resolved, not passed on again, please. This legacy of violent death and its ongoing effects, suppurating in the blood from generation to generation, is it something to do with neglect, with lack of hope, with fear, feeling inadequate, unworthy, isolated?

Is this depression? (Depression (Latin *deprimere*): *to press down*)

Roots feed on dark panic. Generations choke up with fear and insecurity, trapped by a desire to have something to hold on to, to feel safe, someone to hold on to, pulled under by a drowning man. When you are drowning your fear can kill your rescuer – human kindness, benevolence, killed by fear. If you have nothing to lose, trapped by fear and a lack of love, you take others with you, like suicide bombers under the delusion that death will bring all that life and oppressive cultures have denied.

Dad was not always absent for me. One late summer in 1998 he came to stay and we went for a walk up through the woodland onto the mountain that looks back to our old home in Staylittle. We went into a derelict *hafod* (summer farm), with a rusty fridge and quarry tiles stacked near the wall, and half a sheet of polythene stretched over the damp earth floor. We decided to venture upstairs. There was a dank smell of fungi and crumbling stone. The landing is almost as big as the two small bedrooms behind the door. The banisters fence the edge furthest from the window. The windowsill is knee-high. The window is closed. We turn right towards the door, which is half open and streaked with bird shit. The loft door above the entrance is half pushed aside. Then we hear the sound of flapping wings. It is coming from behind the door. I imagine a trapped bird, starving, weak. Dad pushes the door open and suddenly takes a step back. The space is filled by a span of white wings. A barn owl glides past us towards the window. I feel afraid. Its beat of wings skims the skin off the air. Its eyes and beak scan for a way out. Dad surprises me. He moves towards the window, pushes it open and moves back. It is so precise and exactly right that I feel protected. It is so fast that the owl never stops. It takes less time than an owl gliding across eight feet of room. Neither he nor the owl falters.

There is a thud as the owl hits the glass to the left of the open window. It lands on the sill and shuffles along. I can feel its talons scratching the painted wood. It feels the air shimmer outside. It smells the still silk stretching gold and misty, across the mountain to the sky. With hardly a pause the white barn owl, with its wing feathers like autumn leaves, slides off, wafted into nothing, leaving no trace in the air, only the pellets of ground bones and fur, and the shit beneath the loft. I feel less afraid. In that moment Dad is there for me. The owl has broken a stagnant silence, leaving us with less that needs to be said.

In 1968, eight years after my parents divorced, I went to Bristol to re-take two A levels at Filton Tech, before going off to Manchester University in the autumn. I had already dropped out of a teachers' training course, feeling that it wasn't what I wanted to do. It was a time of feeling lost, uncertain and alone. At Christmas, Mum had taken me to the doctor because I couldn't stop crying. He knew about our parents' divorce and I remember telling him about my father crying on the steering wheel of the car. The doctor reassured me that, when my father had asked me if he should come home, that this was a deeply inappropriate question to ask a child. According to the medical record he recommended that I receive some psychoanalysis. My mother neither followed this up nor told me about it.

She seemed unable to face the reality of our father's recently-diagnosed manic depression, or maybe to find a way of talking about it with us. It was another part of the frozen silence.

The disintegration of love, the witnessing of psychological cruelty, the lack of communication, and the emotional insecurity had all wrought an impoverishment within our spiritual life. I would not accept that my father had left our family and that he eventually established another family, or that my mother could not seem to express any of her feelings about this but assumed the mask of a stoical, silent martyr.

It is that place of deep pride that seems to be the most impenetrable form of aggression – the stoical silence that shores up pain into a solid place in which any words would be reaching towards the pain of the thaw. It is easier to stay mute, dumb and numb, deluding yourself that you are beyond reproach. Love had died and left a vacuum of fearful repercussions in its wake.

One way to thaw such cold memories is to share them. In 1973, Lucy and I were trying to understand our parents' divorce during our last time together alone. To learn freshly to love someone who has left (even when you know that you are not in their memory in the same way, if at all), to find a way of loving them during absence, is difficult, but in sharing the vacancy something changed for both of us and memory was modified. Somehow a larger memory allowed liberation from fixed attitudes, or prejudice.

More recently Dad and I have been able to spend more time together again and enjoy each other's company. When the old story of guilt and unresolved pain erupts from the divorce saga, we turn to a favourite phrase, "Well that's just how it is" and somehow this overt, spoken acceptance allows the story to change and dissolve. We have been reclaiming our relationship and healing our memories.

One memory: my hands grip the fresh, scratchy rope of the swing that Dad had made for us, suspended from a high branch of the old apple tree.

All four of us had crowded around him while he burnt two holes through the edges of the wooden seat by using a red hot poker from the nearby bonfire. He had branded the date underneath the seat, with the re-heated poker, before threading the ropes through the holes and knotting them under the seat. Then the thrill of flying up over the gate opening onto the lane, standing up, knees bending and pushing, higher and higher.

Over the years I have also grown closer to Tessa (my father's third wife, and mother of Paul and Julia) although she continues to find it difficult to accept her husband's first family. There are no photographs of us in their home. As a stepmother and a stepdaughter myself, and as the mother of a son and a daughter who have grown up with a stepfather, I continue to live with the painful complexity of these "step" relationships. There are also the "half" relationships. The patterns are intergenerational and ongoing.

Again, I look within. It has been hard for the habits of my unconscious to be free of the loops of two decades of Not Knowing. The mind gets into habits that need dissolving. The rat runs of my mind are no longer an appropriate response. However, dreams bypass rat runs. They try to tell us things, often with great imaginative ingenuity. Dreams have been huge signposts on my journey: from *Pearl*, through Lucy's description of herself "floating free / Like a dream," to my own sleeping visions, the first being the water meadow dream when Lucy told me how to hear the sun move, the second being of her bones. There were three other major ones – now is the time to share the next two, because they shed some light on the frozen silence of Not Knowing.

The third dream was recurrent, a kind of imprint branded in my unconscious. It is the "doll baby dream".

The doll baby is as big/small as my hand. She has no cry. She is as still as a doll, swaddled so it is the face that tells me she is alive, or rather the eyes. The excitement of having a new baby arises when I look at her. Why do I feel that she is a girl? There is no doubt that her flesh is alive and that she is breathing. Her size is disconcerting because it is easy to forget her and then suddenly I remember her but, because she is small, I lose her. She is balanced on my breast, not against the flesh of my breast, but on my shirt. If I could put her in my pocket she might grow like a kangaroo, suckling in my pouch and that way she wouldn't be lost. But she doesn't seem to bend, as if she is almost mummified. The eyes blink and shine. She has no voice. It is easy to forget about her because she doesn't call for me. And she is so small. But when she comes to mind I rush to find her with a dread that she may be dead. But she is always alive and yet she doesn't grow nor shrink. How can I look after her because I don't know how to be her mother? Am I her mother? I don't remember a birth. I see just this perfect porcelain face which breathes and has eyes that stir my heart and make me want to protect and nourish her. But it is so easy to forget her. What makes me remember her with a stabbing panic, remember the feeling of being responsible for her survival? But I don't know how to feed her. And anyway she doesn't grow or shrink. She stays the same and doesn't die when I forget about her. So maybe I'm not her mother after all. But who is she, and why do I forget and remember her as if she is one of my babies? This doll baby is nameless and speaks through her eyes while her cheeks and mouth and brow remain still but warm. If she would open her mouth I would feed her. But she will neither grow nor shrink nor bend. Has she got a body beneath her swaddling? She lies on my breast like an invisible warm brooch. I have borne her for so long. Who is she?

The same night, I had another dream, "The plaster mask that slipped".

Someone was winding a gauze bandage around my head from my chin around my mouth, over my nose up to my eyes. I didn't know who it was and I didn't mind. I watched as if it was a broken arm being set. It didn't affect my breathing at all, although I couldn't speak. Then the plaster went on. Defaced by a cast, I became anonymous, featureless, blank. It was almost a relief. My eyes could receive and give. I could not eat or smell. At some time, the mask slipped and became a support for my neck, like a large dog's collar that my chin rested upon, as if I had a broken neck. It was a mill stone or a clown's ruff. Did my head need to be propped up? From faceless I became neckless, wearing an invisible necklace.

I have written in the previous section of this book about the suffering of the twenty-one years of not knowing what had happened to Lucy. It has been difficult to face the effect upon me of those years. In fact it was not possible until the unearthing. Many people did care for me and reach out, but I pushed them away thinking that I had to rescue myself. Part of me could not grow, was held back, frozen. This is the part that I needed to face and integrate in some way.

The doll baby feels like an elusive, ungraspable mixture of Lucy lost, myself in limbo, a child that was never born, an intergenerational unresolved loss. She is both dead and alive. She is part of me that remains invisible and yet sometimes she needs to be remembered in the dream, and I need to approach her again. The plaster cast dream speaks of a mute paralysis, a desensitization, a willingness to remain in a frozen, impersonal passivity. Together the dreams speak of invisible adornments that remain secret, hidden and in vain. They fetter growth and offer disguise. They are telling me about what needs to become visible, re-membered with love, integrated and dissolved. It is the part that I have needed to confess. I was relieved to read many years later about the death of a child from the sibling's perspective:

The ability of parents to help the siblings communicate within the family unit and the opportunity to directly express feelings lead to a healthy negotiation of grieving tasks.[10]

Communication between my parents and within our family during this period was minimal. An uncontrollable longing for closeness and sexual intimacy took its place, which I had to act upon. My ability to love was inhibited by unresolved, accumulated grief but there was a deep sexual need to "make love" as a way of affirming a sensation of being alive. These compulsive, self-centred actions were about needing to be "in love" as a way of avoiding the emotional paralysis of the backlog of pain, although they were actually deepening the alienation that I felt. Life was changing around me but my life seemed to be frozen. It was difficult to make decisions. There was a strange mixture of creativity and despair, arrogance and fear, shatteredness and selfishness.

Many years later a dear friend apologised for her behaviour at the time. "We just didn't know how to relate to you." This "frozen" life was an involuntary inexpression of the brutal suffering of traumatic, unresolved loss which drove me into a place of exile. I became withdrawn, unapproachable, proud, self-sufficient and yet longing for the company of someone who might understand, longing for a community that could connect with the severance within me.

This extract from my diary of February 1975, one year and two months after Lucy disappeared (which somehow survived and reappeared just when I was ready to read it) describes something of this time and a certain amount of self-reflection and remorse. I had been at a friend's wedding the night before, drunk too much champagne and fallen down some stairs, putting a front tooth through my lower lip.

(Very neat writing in pencil)
Feeling of being disposable; not entirely useless but unwanted, isolated, superfluous, without meaning....Dream of raking through the ghosts, past flesh and spirits.

Puked up clotted milk and champagne at 5 a.m. Everything I did took a long time. Lay on the small bed in a sleeping bag and felt shivery and the wound on my mouth throbbed. Became preoccupied with the wind-change superstition, that if I lay on my side the hole beneath my lip would set crookedly. Also the fear that I may have destroyed the sensitivity in my lips. And the realisation that I won't be able to play the flute for a while. Extreme self-disgust for my lack of self-respect and my lapse into self-destruction, so far from the strength I was feeling a few weeks ago. Set off for the casualty department at the hospital. The hangover felt like the day after a trip: a lot of shit cleared away, but an emptiness which is full of sadness – so much and yet so little to lose. Life, my life, was thrown down the stairs by a body deliberately put out of control by too much alcohol – overweighed with a sense of the responsibility for my own life and the direction it is taking, the waste of time by repeating mistakes and being stuck in the groove of faults not mastered, hemming in the ego, avoiding the possibility of growth and change.

The sun was shining softly, an early morning light so gentle, stroking the earth and the trees. I felt ashamed that I have damaged my own architecture. I cried and found myself praying for forgiveness as I walked along the track between an avenue of beech trees. Speaking is uncomfortable, as is learning about silence and the value of the mouth as a passage for sound, music, food and kisses.

During some research into trauma in the national library in Aberystwyth I came across a sentence that I have long pondered that seems to describe the destruction of not confessing the bits we would rather edit out:

It is not the dead that haunt us but the gaps left within us by the secrets of others.[11]

Secrets live like hungry ghosts inside us. They live on fistfuls of fear. Their mouths gape, their hair-thin necks crane beneath our skin, etiolated; their bellies stretched and empty. They are not gagged but they gag us: choke, retch, strangle, suffocate us. They warp our blood like cancer – a blood which has holes in it, gaps. They keep us from knowing who we are. They shadow us, lurk under rock, fill our bellies with stones, constipate our lives. They keep us safe in their power not to disclose. They silence our song. They drain us with their longing to be told. When is the right time to pierce the skin and erupt: the pus, the blood?

The bits we want to edit out are the bits that the next generation needs to know, if we are going to make any progress in our melting. Blood full of holes passes on to the next generation.

The Not Knowing was not only the loss of Lucy; it was also my own denial, my own ignorance – the way that I didn't see how life really is. I brought up three children during the long Not Knowing, and had several relationships. Every time that I could not hear those parts I would not or could not face, we, the people I was close to, took a step away from the truth. It is so difficult to be truly present as a mother and as a partner. To be truly responsible (response-able) requires an unselfish attitude. Grief is a self-centred process which makes one less compassionate. This unresolved grief meant that something in me was missing for them. Something in my parents was missing for me. If a person goes missing from a family, something in the whole family goes absent. The complete narrative is suspended, but the story goes on in a truncated way. It affects the whole community.

And what about the Wests?

In the final paragraph of Canon David Self's retelling of my story, he recorded some words that had come to me in response to his probing questions:

I feel that I'm most true to myself when I am vulnerable and open to pain. Creativity comes when you have accepted, faced, and experienced the pain. Only then are you free to forgive. When the pain is still unacknowledged or in control, anything you do has the potential to carry negative emotions that destroy. Hatred, anger, rage, vengeance all come from that place of unresolved pain. I think the actions of the Wests come from that place. So I have compassion for them because I know that once you are brutalised, you lose the sense of who you are, the sense of beauty, the sense that God is within you.[12]

Everything that the Wests did to you, Lucy, tells me something about what was done to them in their childhood. It is an expression of the "logic of shame" that James Gilligan talks about in his sensitive study of violence.[13] Their physical acts represent their physical and psychological inheritance.

Please forgive me, Lucy, if I begin to look at you in this way. I am now looking at you as their victim, on a physical level: no mouth, no voice, no clothes, just the flesh and bones that were used for sexual gratification. The Wests used their own children (physical extensions that they "created"), destructively ignorant of their unique individual being. I can find the verbs for the actions of the Wests, but adjectives and adverbs seem excessive. The verb carries enough sensation. You became the object of the damage that the Wests experienced in their childhood. Your body became a literal object and your extreme physical pain registered the depth of their impotent, inarticulate rage, of their grief and shame. Words failed.

From the moment that we learnt the violent, grotesque details surrounding your death, I have been struggling to understand the roots of the Wests' behaviour. There is no going back. It has changed us all in different ways. Sadly, joyfully, we are all the better (and the worse) for it, because it strikes the bedrock of the experience of being alive as a human being. It has forced me open to the reality of the cycle of violence and abuse that taints and warps us all in subtle and extreme ways. It was an undercurrent in our childhood too. We were dismembered by divorce, gagged by a mixture of separated parents and adolescence. Now I am filled with a passion to find a way out of this cycle, for the sake of our children's future.

The Wests abducted you, either by force or deception. (Who abducted their childhood?) By that time Rosemary had three children, Heather, Mae, Stephen (four months old), and one older stepdaughter, Anne-Marie. Charmaine, the other stepdaughter, was already murdered. Rose told a neighbour that Charmaine had gone back to her mother, Rena Costello, and added, "bloody good riddance". By that time, Rena (also Anne-Marie's mother) was also already dead.

The Wests stole you from us. (Who stole them? Or who didn't miss them when they had gone?) They punched you. Your front tooth, capped after a hockey ball had knocked it out, was missing from your skull. They gagged you. (Who wouldn't let them speak? Who didn't listen to them? How early were they silenced? When was their truth negated? When did they become in-valid?) They strung you up and raped you. Were you conscious or unconscious from now on? (Who immobilised them and played with them as sexual objects?) Did they kill you directly or did you die alone? (Who killed them, and their sense of a sacred self?) They dismembered you and decapitated you. (Who fragmented them and demolished them?) They disarticulated your joints. (Why were they emotionally inarticulate?)

One of Canon David Self's definitions of "sin" resonates with me:

Sin is a proud claim to be self-sufficient in life, claiming a total freedom for ourselves and the way we live.[14]

This definition highlights that which needs to be healed within us in order to know wholeness, to be able to live in community with each other. Confessing our "sins" allows a movement from feelings that are isolating, corrosive and thus potentially harmful and shrinking, towards something that connects us with the whole of humanity. It can be an act which brings release and vitality and opens up the possibility of being forgiven (freed from the bitterness and hatred of others or one's denigrating, shrunken self). It is unburdening and enlightening. It is affirming of a larger sense of "self", free from the pride of self-sufficiency, closer to the ground of our being.

Chapter 6

FINDING A VOICE

The frozen silence was carried for three decades. It held all that was put on hold during the years of Not Knowing. Darkness was welling up within my unconscious. When an iceberg melts the visible surface of ice above the water line is sometimes striped with parallel, horizontal rings. These rings are gnawed by the impact of the sea and the loose ice on the circumference of the iceberg, while it is slapped and sucked by the waves. When the iceberg melts the mass of ice gets lighter and this form rises up out of the sea, with its rings. It was as if the huge, necessary melting within me was glinting in the ring of the iceberg. Sometimes I heard the sound of the sun moving, of ice dissolving into water: an ominous creaking, a melting, a lightening. This gleaming girdle rose into view, gouged and glistening with thawed words, as the ice melted.

Professing is another aspect of confessing. To profess, I give voice to what arises. All that was trapped in the frozen silence calls out to be reclaimed and acknowledged. I give voice to that which affirms and feeds us and gives us the faith to continue.

Pro- (prefix) *forth, out forward, towards the front, into a public position*

Shortly after wrapping Lucy's bones, I felt her near me. Perhaps it was in the realms of a visitation. It was as if she were standing above me on a cloud with her feet astride. Her feet were visible and grounded, not swirled about by the cloud. And yet the cloud was not solid. She was wearing a knee-length, white toga. Her legs and feet were bare. She appeared like a mixture of an Amazon and an angel. Her hair was gold and frizzier than ever. In one hand she was holding a long flaming torch, swung away from her hip like a shepherd's crook or a staff. Her face was smiling and she was no longer wearing spectacles. In a way that could only be Lucy's, she was telling me, firmly and clearly: "Just get on with it, Marian."

As my children grew closer to the age when you disappeared, Lucy, I felt an obsessive desire to pay tribute to your life, to be allowed to remember you within our family, to show my love for you, to have a spoken memory of you in my life again. The feeling became more urgent. Something was about to burst open, like a thorn working its way towards the surface. Finding words, writing, became one approach in my search for meaning.

The words that arose within me came from an instinctive need for a terrible truth to survive, a bearing of witness, a speaking by proxy in the face of unspeakable demolition. If I had tried to carry on with no words I would have allowed death. That kind of dying is too common, especially amongst women. Not speaking because of fear of the consequences. Not speaking because of a feeling of inadequacy. Not speaking because there don't seem to be any words there. Just a frozen silence. If only Rosemary West could have spoken and been heard, could speak and be heard.

The Italian-Jewish writer and chemist, Primo Levi, wrote about his experience of this need to "speak by proxy" after living through and surviving his time in Auschwitz III (Monowitz Nazi concentration camp):

those who saw the Gorgon have not returned to tell about it, or have returned mute... we speak in their stead, by proxy. I could not say whether we did so or do so because of a kind of moral obligation towards those who were silenced, or rather in order to

*free ourselves of their memory; certainly we did it because of a
strong and durable impulse. I do not believe that psychoanalysts
(who have pounced upon our tangles with professional avidity) are
competent to explain the impulse...*

*Perhaps it would be more correct to see it as an atavistic
anguish whose echo one hears in the second verse of Genesis...*[15]

And the earth was without form, and void; and darkness was
upon the face of the deep. And the Spirit of God moved upon the
face of the waters.[16]

Anguish: (from the French *angoisse*) *choking*, (from the
Latin *angustia*) *tightness*, (from *angustus*) *narrow*.

From a tightening, a narrowing, the eye of a needle, to a
great opening. From a constricted, sore throat (which I had
for the whole of the Rosemary West trial) to speech. What
needed to be reclaimed and acknowledged rushed through like
a spring flood gushing into a water meadow, bringing renewal.
Its pace was sure and unfaltering. Some people said that Lucy
"had a hand in writing it". I certainly learnt more about our
relationship as the images and memories arrived. I began to
feel as if we shared a sacred realm, that we had both longed to
know. "The point of intersection of the timeless with time",
from T.S. Eliot's The Dry Salvages (Section V) in *Four Quartets*
that we used to contemplate and muse about, had made itself
known. This is where we are truly akin.

The gag had to dissolve. The words did come back. Your
voice in mine. Mine in yours. We did it. The prayer flags and
the Yevtushenko poem entwined. The words and images that
arise when "you" (your little self) has been dropped, in the
midst of disaster, aren't "yours" even if you wrote them down.
This love cannot stay still, nor wait. It is a gift that needs to be
shared. This is the territory of *Pearl*.

Why and how did I write? It was clear that the experience of
traumatic loss required honouring with time and serious effort
so that the legacy of unresolved pain could be transformed, so
that less would be passed on to the next generation. I allowed
one day a week to sit with whatever arose in my mind and write

it down. Writing became a way of allowing myself time and solitude to experience my grief, by finding words and images as a structure for my own healing. Its direction was informed by meditation and prayer. There were days when the words were nowhere to be seen and the sky was dark.

Each word felt like a rung on a ladder leading from a deep pit. Sometimes I felt that I was risking the disintegration of myself without the assurance that a new whole would emerge. But I did not seem to have the choice to turn back. Gradually, I found trust in this as part of the process of creativity and healing. I was rescuing and reclaiming something of Lucy's truth and finding a depth of compassion that I had never known. I was beginning to trust that I would be given what I needed in order to fulfil a vow that I had made to try and bring something positive out of this apparent demolition.

My voice had returned like a solitary, migrant bird, flying across the decades of frozen silence. My truth, our truth. Not just us as sisters but us as women in search of meaning with common family roots in a culture that seethes with all that we would prefer to edit out: paedophilia, serial killing, trafficking of women, drug and alcohol abuse, greed, poverty and a hypocritical veneer of democracy.

The writing started in December 1995. After five months it stopped, it was printed out and cut up. The shape came as I shuffled the images around on the floor. The words had arrived and fallen into place. But there was still no title. During the period of writing there was a serious, ecological disaster. An oil tanker, *The Sea Empress*, burst its contents into the sea near Milford Haven. This was the coastline of our childhood holidays, and of family holidays with our children. The media images were of seabirds blackened and glued-shut with crude oil, beaches gagged with a black adhesion. "The West victims" had been gummed-up, and stained. Your lives, your voices, had been gagged and dismembered. The rescue work was called "salvage": reclaiming the birds, the sea life, the beaches, and the sea from this toxic, suffocating death. There was a resonance. The title of my first piece about Lucy had arrived: *Salvaging the Sacred*.

Sacred refers to that which helps take us out of our little selves into the larger self of the whole universe.[17]

Putting the words "out there" was one of the most exacting decisions I have ever made. It felt as if I was leaving the rest of the family behind and risking losing them. As if they were on an island and I was in a small boat rowing towards a larger island with something that needed to be heard. It felt as if I was cutting through the umbilical cord of my "kin", as an adult in my own right, to reclaim my lost "kin", my sister. This act was towards trusting a greater "kynde", a greater community. It was empowering, terrifying and vitally necessary.

A friend suggested that maybe I was building a bridge between the two islands and that the family could follow when they were ready. It took Mum eight years before she read the essay. Dad read it immediately and was the first relative to get in touch. He said that he found it really helpful. I don't think either of my brothers has read it. If they have, they never responded. I know that some of their unresolved pain was projected onto me at times. But I could only stay true to my own path. I had remembered my brother David saying that everyone would think that Lucy was just "your average teenage girl loitering around in a mini skirt".

It was sad for me because I was convinced that I was doing it for the whole family. It took me quite a while to accept that each family member had a right to his/her own way of grieving, and that my way might be threatening theirs. These are the rifts that tear families apart. Yet we have all been enlarged by the sharing of the words. We were enabled to talk more openly about our feelings and our attempts to accept and let go in some way, about our differing ways forward.

On 18th May 1996 *Salvaging the Sacred* was published in the *Guardian Weekend* after weeks of careful, sensitive communication with the editor at that time, Deborah Orr. Her respect for the words and the way in which they went "out there" helped to heal some of the trauma of the media onslaught. It was an empowering experience. On that day our family went to a local May festival in Newtown. I was unnerved and excited to see people carrying you around. The cropped black and white image of you filled the cover of the *Guardian Weekend* with the words "Lucy, my Sister". Your face was folded under people's arms, spread out on benches, fluttering in the wind. It was especially gratifying to open the magazine and see the image that was used while you were out there as a "missing person" and then as a "West victim", restored to colour and placed back into its original context, next to me with the weathered columns of Rievaulx Abbey framing us.

For the first two years after the unearthing we were plunged into the powerful rapids of the thaw, each of us finding his or her way to stay afloat. However, under the turbulence was a wonderful surprise: a huge lake of warmth and compassion glowing, lapping, gently sustaining. It continues even now, in various ways: sometimes in the material form of letters, phone calls, conversations, hugs. Sometimes it is less tangible but is to do with the best in humanity, the choice to send love in thoughts and prayers.

It became clear through the writing that the closer I got to accepting Lucy's death, the more I could remember about our rich childhood.

Images came floating back. My memory did not seem to filter out or separate into "good and bad"; the images simply resurfaced in a way that formed a strangely paradoxical dream-like world. The memories of this landscape of our childhood needed to emerge and be acknowledged before they dissolved and receded. When I wrote them down, they stood without judgment. They were simply what came back. They held an innocence, and felt like a gift to be shared.

We grew up in a converted cider mill in the middle of a Cotswold village. Lucy, I remember you trying to paint pictures of the bantam cockerels that strutted and crowed throughout our childhood at The Mill; the Chinese geese that hissed and laid huge eggs that we made Mark collect from the back of the house; the duck called "C" that laid sea-green eggs under the St. John's wort on the bank around the pond. Our bedrooms, where the apples used to be stored, were small with thick walls and tiny windows. Sometimes we would roast some of the abundant supply of cider apples from the orchard on sticks, watching the juice spit in the flames and the skins bubble and blacken. Sometimes we would crush the apples in one of the cider presses making the juice trickle around the stone groove which was patterned with yellow lichens. This brew was known as "Black Lady" and we would take it in turns to sip the sour, gritty liquid as if it was a rare elixir. We often played games to do with getting around the Big Room without touching the ground. We had the freedom to explore the hill, making slides in the woods and swinging off creepers. We skidded around the courtyard on tricycles, veering onto two wheels around the sharpest corner past the lavender bush. There was a perfume of lavender and wallflowers in the summer and the sound of the pressure-cooker hissing with soup or stew. We had a raft made of oil cans from nearby Gretton Farm and planks of wood which provided endless entertainment on the pond, ranging from timeless contemplation of newts, lying on our fronts gazing into the muddy water, to rougher battles which usually ended up with someone falling in. The smell of that muddy, weedy water remains in my memory.

After a massacre of guinea pigs by a fox, Lucy carefully buried each mauled corpse. A close childhood friend told us about another incident with a dead guinea pig.

I was scared to kiss him as he was dead. Lucy was very angry with me. She told me fiercely that just because something dies it doesn't mean that you should stop loving it and that everyone deserves to be kissed before going to heaven.

In our teenage years we spent less time doing things together. *Murder in the Dark* and *Postman's Knock* were always popular games to play with our cousins and local village friends as we moved into adolescence. Riding our pony, Felix, on the hill was a daily activity. Lucy always seemed to be copying what I was doing (like learning the viola), which was irritating. Actually she was going her own way and writing sophisticated poetry.

It was not only with the spoken and written word that the frozen silence was negotiated and thawed. Very soon after Lucy's disappearance, in 1975, I began to learn *Tai Chi*, discovering the importance of listening to my body and of learning about the subtle energies that can become trapped and cause disease (*dis*-ease). The body remembers trauma in every cell and needs to find its voice, its release, through movement. It needs to be strengthened in its openness and flexibility, its ability to be alert and alive in response to whatever arises. *Tai Chi* reminded me of the importance of being kind to myself, to this unique embodiment of life. It was a form of professing the body with others, of transforming that which is stagnant and blocked.

From my diary, 5th February 1975:
Deep change from the lethargic despondency of this morning. Why? The Tai Chi session today was extra block-dispersing. The theme we explored today in the exercises was directly related to the fact (as proved today in my experience) that fatigue is basically to do with blocked energy. So apart from the spine stretching exercise we did a breathing through the block/pain exercise... pain replaced by heat... replaced by pain... etc. through the layers of resistance... breathing oneself into the area four finger-widths below the navel... great feeling of a shifting from my head downwards and a warm, sexy glow in my abdomen.

Tai Chi was my first encounter with an Eastern holistic practice. This slow-moving meditation is about becoming "as still as a mountain" and moving "like a great river". It originated from a Taoist monk, Chang San-feng, who lived in China from 1279–1368 CE (approximately 100 years before the writing of *Pearl*). Each movement is grounded in the observation of natural movements within all forms of life (for example the exchange of energy between a crane fighting with a snake). It embodies the principles of becoming deeply rooted and knowing the strength that comes from "yielding" to another's energy and yet maintaining contact with it, "sticking", in order to uproot the opponent.

This is something that I have continued to practise throughout my life. It has been an essential contribution to my physical, emotional and spiritual health. It is through this practice that I moved to Wales three years later. In 1976 I had taken a holiday in the Welsh cottage belonging to my friend Barbara (who was to become my Tai Chi teacher and acupuncturist), and discovered a farmhouse of my own to rent further up the mountain. The children and I finally left London, to live permanently in Wales, in 1979.

From my diary, Sunday 9th February 1975:
...feeling alive again. Definite spring sunshine, mist and Turnerish mimosa. Tai Chi today. We learnt "Embrace Tiger and return to Mountain". The Mountain means "keeping still".

The 1975 diary is full of the vigour and creativity of this time even though I was deep in the Not Knowing. I was also learning, exploring, and experiencing new ways forward. In retrospect this is warming and amusing but also astonishing in the realisation of the grace that upheld me and didn't forsake me.

Later that year I came across the practice of homeopathy which gradually became my "profession". I was pregnant with my first child, Luke. A friend who was studying this alternative medicine wanted a pregnant woman to treat so I became his guinea pig. I was so impressed by the gentle, permanent change in my health (mental, emotional and physical) during this treatment that I converted my approach to health from then onwards.

Soon after Marigold was born, in 1979, I was living in the remote farmhouse in mid-Wales. I decided that I needed to study homeopathy in order to be able to treat my own children (there were no practising homeopaths in the area then) I began a three-year course of study in Devon, one weekend a month, with Misha Norland.

Those weekends were healing in themselves as we explored and shared together. I graduated in 1984, after my third child, Jack, was born. By this time I realised that there was an increasing need for a qualified homeopath in the area so I set up my clinic in Llanidloes. Local demand led to me working once a fortnight in a friend's home in Llandrindod Wells, and later in the Rock Park Clinic and the Harbourside Clinic in Porthmadog.

Although homeopathy is at times attacked and discredited in the media by various medical professionals, my experience of this subtle approach to health continues to inspire me and improve the health of my clients. Dr. Samuel Hahnemann (1755–1843), the German founder of homeopathy, was horrified by the brutality and results of the medical practices of his time (especially blood letting). He turned away from it and began to earn his living as a translator, which led to his discovery of the law of "like curing like".

While translating a book entitled *Materia Medica,* he came across the detail that cinchona bark seemed to be effective in the cure of malaria. He ingested some of the bark and was astonished to find that he developed the symptoms of malaria. This initiated years of painstaking provings of other substances, during which the mental, emotional and physical symptoms produced in the healthy prover were recorded and collated into a picture of a remedy. He also began to potentise his remedies through a process of dilution and succussion. The less of the substance, the more the succussion, the more the potency. The vital force of life (the *qi* in Chinese medicine) is seen as that which needs to be re-balanced by the remedy.

His description of health, from paragraph 9 of *The Organon of Medicine*, remains the goal of my profession:

In the healthy condition of man, the spiritual force (autocracy), the dynamis that animates the material body (organism), rules with unbounded sway, and retains all the parts of the organism in admirable, harmonious, vital operation, as regards both sensations and functions, so that our indwelling, reason-gifted mind can freely employ this living, healthy instrument for the higher purposes of our existence.[18]

In my own work as a homeopath, I have listened to other people's pain, suffering and illness and have witnessed their healing processes. There have been many private confessions. This holistic perspective has informed my work in prisons.

It has also made me intensely aware of the need to get in touch with, and express in some way, the dark pain in our lives, in order not to become stuck in negative, destructive emotions.

Serious physical and mental pathology can develop as a direct result of this denial.

I also profess a deep commitment towards, and faith in, the discipline, teachings, practice and support of my Quaker and Chan Buddhist communities. I will explore this aspect of my narrative of healing more fully in *Comprehending*, the next section of the book. But simply to say that it is within the compelling silence of nature, in solitude or shared silence, that I was enabled to look within. From this ground it was possible to sometimes share with others who are also committed to searching within for a place of belonging, without avoiding the thaw of that which we would prefer to edit out or bypass.

My experience of moving towards acceptance and understanding involves an enlarging of context, and a painful acknowledgement of my own guilt, my own part in wrongdoing and the acknowledgement of its effect upon others. This way involves a movement from the self-centred perspective towards one which is open to being changed and enlarged in some way, made whole (as the root of its word suggests: Old Saxon hal, hale: *whole*. The words health and holy also have this root). This is where I have found strength and refuge.

This change of attitude involves a process of purification that could be called "sweeping invisible dust". By attending to what is required in this present moment, wholeheartedly, lightheartedly, and generous-heartedly, the invisible dust of the past, the negative habits, the destructive emotions, all that is "spotted" begins to dissolve, as a more spacious connection with the present moment arises.

In 2004 I attended one of the many silent retreats, or shared spaces for contemplation, which had by then become an integral part of my path. My retreat job was to clean a wide, empty room at the top of the large house. On first glance it looked clean enough. But the sweeping of invisible dust began with smiling, as the broom handle extended from my navel and led me across the floor from one side of the room to the other, pausing at the inner wall, stooping to sweep the invisible dust into a dustpan. Slowly turning around, I swept back towards the windows, aiming for the radiators, measuring the beginning of the line with the width of the dustpan.

Outside, the tip of the ancient cedar swayed gracefully in the storm, howling and lashing against the sash windows, which seemed to stutter in their frames. From side to side the broom travelled, leading me forward. It was as if my life depended upon sweeping the floor with devout attention. Somehow it did. I was smiling because that was all that was to be done in that moment. By accepting that, there was fulfilment. By accepting the discipline of the practice and giving my full attention to each stuck, painful emotion, one after the other, the dust is swept away.

In the grounds outside there is a stream that sings of wisdom and clarity, sweeping aside the noisy, grasping thoughts that block its way like sticks clotted with trapped, dead leaves: thoughts and anxieties which eddy about, frittering in circles on the edges, ignoring, holding back from the surging current. This stream is free from worry, as it sings of the broom that sweeps invisible dust, insisting that true life depends upon it. Please help me to bow with humility and gratitude. Please accept what can be offered now. Here is a pine branch torn down by the storm. It is offered to the fire that crackles and bursts into flames full of love, its smoke rising with the incense of prayer that moves in the wake of the broom.

Comprehending

Chapter 7

PEELING AWAY THE LAYERS

In the autumn of 2003 I went on my first solitary retreat. I planned to find a balance between meditation and writing and was hoping to make progress with the elusive shape of "the book". I opened a file entitled "Dream Vision" which was stuffed with various notes, thoughts and correspondence. Unexpectedly I came across a single page, torn out of a spiral bound notebook. It was the original page from my diary in 1994 describing the skeleton dream which had been recorded the following morning.

It was astonishing to read, almost ten years after the dream, a detail that I had never paid attention to before.

Next thing I know –they [Lucy's bones] were all assembled into a complete skeleton – which I embraced, the skull resting on my shoulder – then she started to talk to me. It felt very natural and I wanted to hold her for ever – perhaps I can.

From my diary, October 2003:

Monday evening. Colder. Felt like making a fire in the sitting room. Found kindling in the cowsheds and coal. I bring my cushion downstairs for an evening sit.

I end up lying down, relaxing, absorbing the warmth and patterns of the flames. I remember the dead in our family and friends. My stepfather's corpse came to mind and I cried a little. Letting go, letting go as the fire burnt down and the embers shrunk. I lay listening to the flames. They sound like cloth flapping at times. Like sheets drying in the wind. Like the wind catching in the canvas of a sail.

The idea of using the structure of the medieval dream vision for the book, and somehow having a conversation between me (the Dreamer) and Lucy (the Pearl Maiden) began to form. How would this dialogue come about? In the skeleton dream Lucy had spoken to me. What did she say? In my mind there was a taboo against fictionalising anything to do with Lucy's "truth" (which had been so distorted by the Wests and the media). My efforts had been to reclaim her from these pollutions. But it felt liberating to realise that an imagined conversation with Lucy could be a way of integrating and clarifying our relationship and releasing us from our joint identity in the media. But it was impossible, for some time, to know how to start it. The dialogue that follows, which took place when I had almost given up on the idea, surprised me and made me aware of the complexity of this bereavement. It helped me to accept the loss.

Lucy: *I told you to just get on with it ages ago! You were free to do whatever you chose then, but you worried away, wanting to "bring something positive" out of my death. You wanted to finish your book. You are obliged, for your own sake (forget about me) to finish this book. This is your last chance. Twelve years have passed. So what is keeping you from finishing it?*

Marian: *I'm not used to you being bossy – even ungrateful. I didn't expect you to be losing patience too. Does it make a difference to you when or whether I finish it? I thought that you had all the time out of this world. I've been waiting nine months to know how to start this dialogue, and then you just butt in with an exasperated explosion.*

Lucy: *Your time is running out. I can see you going under. You must accept by now that life never turns out how you imagine it or plan it. Never. You can't keep waiting for it to be perfect and all worked out neatly. But we should have already learnt that from our parents' divorce. Sometimes human love disintegrates. We lose heart. We lose faith. We get lost. We all have to die. We know that much is true. But we also know moments of perfection that inspire us towards that place where who we thought we were drops away and we know that we are interconnected with all forms of life. You are searching too hard. You are too hard on yourself. Learn to be kinder to yourself and then you can be kinder to everyone else. I would like to be your guest again but I have to go now. I can't wait for you to finish. I died in 1973.*

Marian: *It seems that as soon as I feel as if I have understood something about myself the next layer of unresolved pain looks me in the eye, as if I am sabotaging my aspirations by thinking I have arrived somewhere safe and clear. That this process of healing never ends and just when I think I've worked something out the next crisis kicks in, testing where I am all over again, offering more opportunity for change and learning more about who I am: layer after layer, grief, rage, fear in various mixtures of confusion, with an occasional glimpse of a purer place that leaves as soon as I try to grasp it. The "it" is a bit like my memory of your essential purity, that seems to continue and grow within me when I stop trying to remember it.*

Lucy: *Don't be so hard on yourself. I thought I was the procrastinator, the perfectionist, the scholar, the aesthete, the poet, in search of all that is good, true and virtuous. My death was seemingly out of keeping with my profession. My earthly aspirations, who I was hoping to become, have long* gone. *Besides, all this is holding you back from living – from the living who need you more than I have ever done. I'm not being ungrateful. It's time to be honest. I have to go. I sent you the results of my faith, the "peace that passeth understanding", the place where "if you sit very still you can hear the sun move". Now you must find that place in yourself. That is where you can feel safe, strong and true to your own life, where you care and cure, trust and triumph. The main clue that you don't seem to be getting is that it is beyond understanding: it is the "light that shines in the darkness, and the darkness comprehendeth it not."*

Marian: *What happened to you is beyond understanding. Now I feel really confused. It's all very well telling me to "just get on with it", from wherever you are, but I have been trying to take this seriously. Please don't leave me now. Look, it's taken up nine more years of my life and it has to be right. I really do want to finish it. I'm sick to death of it. But extricating myself from our public persona, resuming my life without you (from "Lucy Partington's sister, Marian", to "Marian Partington, and who is she?") and before that trying not to forget you for twenty years while you were out there as "a missing person". I was always scanning, waking up with a heavy feeling that it wasn't real. Have I tried to make you into a Heavenly Sister in your death, and idealised you? You can't stop me from doing that. I have to get there in my own time, surrender, renounce, although you can warn me that time is running out. Keep challenging me, like a Zen Mistress. I had hoped to write us both into that place: lotus sisters, with occasional visits from you as my guest, reminding me of what matters in life and death, reminding me of eternity.*

Lucy: *Well, I'm glad I butted in before that happened.*

Marian: *You are right. The lesson was there the second you disappeared. I had to face the reality that someone you love can be talking to you, go out for the evening saying goodbye, and never come back, leaving – and then the Not Knowing for twenty years. Where does that leave me? Where does it leave you? When does it leave me?*

Lucy: *The Weather in the Duck Pond*
When the pond is ice
It is not very nice.
When there is snow,
In a duck house they go
But warm is the sun,
When the summer's begun.

Marian: *We were trying to work something out together before we moved out into adulthood. I'm not sure when I did attain that status. Have I? Adulthood is something about responsibility. I have to reach a compromise between what is demanded of me within my family relationships (as a mother, partner, sister, cousin, aunt, niece, daughter) and what calls me, what I am led towards as a unique individual – when I allow myself to be unravelled and re-knitted.*

Lucy: *But now that you know something of the truth about my disappearance (certainly not all of it) you can be free to live your life without that residue of pain.*

Marian: *It has taken so long, just to face and accept the horror of your death and then to face and accept that we will probably never know exactly how and when you died. And then to face and accept the loss within all those years of not knowing where you were. It has taken so long to realise that letting go with love can bring hope and renewal. And then there is the actualisation – allowing the place where that can happen, deep inside. Maybe this separation, when you leave this time, can be less violent? If you can only hang on until I have said enough. I need you to hear me. You can have the last word.*

Lucy: *When you have found your true self you have found me and then we are part of everything, at "the intersection of time with eternity"…If you think it will help you, I will listen. But I have already gone and we are already free!*

The movement towards comprehension is neither logical nor straightforward. Essentially it involves becoming less self-centred, which makes space for the experience of empathy for oneself and others. It also involves sitting still within the mystery beyond human comprehension. It involves getting out of the way. Ultimately, it may involve becoming forgiving.

Transformative forgiveness…is not a crescendo movement or a linear development; it is rather a fluctuating, unpredictable, and difficult process: "You hit on it, you get a taste of it, and then you take two or three steps back; you get back on the path again and then you fall off again.[19]

My task is to peel away, over and over again, all that keeps me from receiving and giving love, from knowing my "kynde", my interconnection with all things.

I attended my first Buddhist retreat in May 1994, a month after I wrapped Lucy's bones. It was there that I met my Buddhist teacher, Dr. John Crook, founder of the Western Chan Fellowship.[20] My husband had overheard him enquiring about books on Tibet in our local bookshop and felt drawn towards him. A conversation revealed that he led retreats in Wales, and Nick and I booked into a Western Zen retreat shortly before we found out what had happened to Lucy. Then we found ourselves in the midst of the traumatic events of March 1994. Fortunately John encouraged us to go ahead with the retreat.

The retreat centre, Maenllwyd (grey rock) turned out to be surprisingly near to our home. The small Welsh farmhouse stands at the end of a rough track at the lower end of a narrow, wooded valley, just below the horizon of the hill, barely visible from the road below. It is secluded, ascetic and humble, with no electricity, just sitting there amidst the fields of sheep, aloof from the small, straggly village below. The eastern horizon offers wide skies for the sunrise and a distant view of hills across the valley. There are cries of buzzards and crows, the astonishing circling and swooping of red kites, occasional foxes, a burbling stream which keeps the milk cool, and a farmyard which is in turns dusty or muddy.

Inside, the firelight and Tilley lamps bring a flickering glow to the low beams which are hung with various objects that seem to have been there for decades amidst the cobwebs. Dusty prayer flags and a pair of snow shoes, criss-crossed with sinews, attract my attention. There is a sound of tea being poured into mugs, steam rising amidst the quiet arrival of retreatants. We are asked why we have come, what are we looking for? This is just the place I needed. It has offered many people a refuge for contemplation and self-confrontation. Yet we had never come across it until now. It felt safe and exciting, free from pretension or preoccupation with external fuss.

Here I was free to sit very still in silent meditation with a group of other seekers, to investigate and remain true to whatever arose within me, without the distractions of my busy life at home. There was a demanding, disciplined, daily schedule, beginning at 4.30 a.m. and ending at 9.30 p.m. The retreat offered a perfect balance of Buddhist teachings, periods of meditation, personal interviews with the teacher, work periods, walks and wonderful vegetarian meals. This safe, freeing structure became an essential part of my search for comprehension and healing.

At first, arranging work, family and finance before going away, out of all communication, for six days, created a conflict. I was pursuing something that felt vital for my own life, and beneficial to others. Yet I felt trapped by a sense of guilt about leaving the family. I wanted everything to be in order before I left. It was like preparing to give birth.

John Crook changed my life in a radical way by suggesting that the more I shared of my experience the more I would be helping others.

The structure and method of this first retreat, known as Western Zen, had been devised by John. It is a balance of silent meditation and co-counselling sessions (communication exercises). Each participant is given a question to work with, for example, "Who am I?" During the communication exercises, retreatants work in pairs for half an hour. For the first five minutes one person asks the other to "answer" the question that they are working with and simply listens in silence without response. The roles are reversed for the next five minutes. Then the partners change and the process continues. By "emptying out the barrel" of who one thought one was, a liberating, relaxed spacious way of being arises, allowing one to become more integrated with all that is arising in the present moment.

John's response to my very recent experience of wrapping Lucy's bones was deeply respectful. His authentic lack of judgement and deep listening created a feeling of safety and space to be true to whatever was arising in that moment. One of the first Tibetan artefacts that I saw at the retreat centre was a human thigh bone with a silver mouth piece. At the time this resonated with my experience of Lucy's bones. Transforming this long bone into a ceremonial instrument seemed like a perfect creative act. Later someone told me that the bone would probably have come from a criminal and that blowing through this bone was thought to be healing. To engage with compassion in such a direct way cut through some more of my prejudice and opened my imagination.

John also introduced me to my first bodhisattva,[21] Ksitigarbha, who chose to remain on earth as long as there are people in the hell realm who need liberating. His vow includes this sentence: "If I do not go to hell to help the suffering beings there, who else will go?" The statue of this "wisdom being" was deeply moving to me at that time. He holds a staff to break open the gates of hell and a wish-fulfilling jewel to light up the darkness. Both John and Ksitigarbha connected with my suffering in a way that left me feeling heard. I learnt later that Ksitigarbha is the patron deity of deceased children and aborted foetuses in Japan.

Just over a year later, in June 1995, Chan Master Sheng Yen, founder of the Dharma Drum Mountain Association in Taiwan, was to come to Wales to lead a retreat. He was John Crook's teacher and had appointed John to become his Dharma Heir in the West. This was his third visit to Wales and to Maenllwyd.

Master Sheng Yen dedicated his life to the practice of Chan (Chinese Zen), which originated in China in the 6th century CE. His life as a young monk, and later as a Master, was lived with deep devotion during the turmoil of the religious and political upheavals in mainland China. It is with deep gratitude that I recall this auspicious retreat with the inspiring monk who was an international Chan Master. Like John Crook, his influence in my life was transforming.

A place became free on the retreat just two weeks before it began. My daughter was especially generous in her encouragement of me to go, despite the fact that it was during the week of some of her GCSE exams. "You must go Mum."

We were camping outside, washing in the stream, while beyond the field on a distant bank foxes with young cubs played in the sun. On this retreat my questions were focussed upon the need to learn more about humility and gratitude. My destructive habit of criticising others (from a defensive place of arrogance) was having a negative effect upon myself and others. My pride was isolating, restrictive and selfish. How to be able truly to say that I am sorry, how to be able to say thank you, how to be able to forgive myself and others? It seemed to boil down to how to reduce my ego or find a new relationship with myself which was less separate and more connected.

As the week's retreat unfolded a deepening sense of faith strengthened me. Talks by Shifu (which is the Chinese word for teacher, the name we gave to Master Sheng Yen) were on the areas of my inner life that needed to be faced and investigated. The very questions arising unspoken in me were answered by his teachings. It was a bit like the process in Quaker Meetings. My early experience of Meetings in 1987, sitting in a circle with others in silence for an hour, soon convinced me that there was more going on than just a bit of peace and quiet. When people stood up to "give ministry" their words were always in answer to where I was in myself at that moment.

To illustrate the importance of humility, Shifu told us a story about a Chan Master who dedicated his life to Chan practice and, at the age of 120 years, claimed to be just beginning. It was something to do with patience and openness to learning. His talk on gratitude clarified a lesson which had begun to take root on John's retreats: to be grateful for whatever life brings, especially to those who cause you pain or humiliate you. Every moment offers a chance to learn more about compassion or empathy with the suffering of one's "enemy" (one's humiliator). He said that it is necessary to investigate what it is about oneself and about them that fuelled this moment. One has to cultivate another attitude of mind ("weed out the seeds of war within", as the Quakers would say).

During a session of prostrations, we practised repentance. Memories flowed into me about times when I have hurt others and hidden behind my pride. Surrendering my whole life, in body, thought and mind, bowing with my forehead to the ground, giving myself up and all that keeps me from forgiving, surrendering. An insight arises about how I might free myself from this deepening silt of past mistakes. Here is a method of confessing that seems to work. As I bow to the earth my cheeks begin to relax more. The mask on my face begins to drop. That mask is following the gravity of grief, the pulling back to the earth. Just let the mask drop away like dew evaporating in the sun, tea seeping into hot water, a leaf falling in the wind: let me know my real face. Was the "plaster mask" dream about this too? Two feelings follow repenting: gratitude for the sacredness of my life, and a sense of connection with others.

It was possible in that moment to make a strong resolution at least to aim to forgive the Wests, the people who abducted, raped, tortured and murdered my dear sister. I wrote:

I believe this aim, which is the deepest vow I have ever made, will lead to the opportunity to be able to do this one day.

But how?

At the end of the retreat I chose to receive the transmission of the three refuges from Chan Master Sheng Yen: refuge in the Buddha, in the Dharma (Buddhist teachings) and the Sangha (spiritual community). My Dharma name was given: *Guo Guang* which means "result of light". So now my spiritual path was dual. Fortunately, Quakers are rooted in Christianity but also "open to new sources of Light from wherever they may come". Both disciplines, communities and teachings/ experiences informed and strengthened my way forward. To have the "refuge" of both the Buddha and Christ allowed me to travel on and deepen my knowledge of faith, hope and love. For me, both paths move towards an authentic experience of being less self-centred and more engaged with everyday life.

They seem to be inter-related and ultimately they meet beyond identity.

The day after the retreat ended, I experienced murderous rage. It seemed to come out of nowhere, rushing up from my navel, dashing its heat and power against the inside of my skull, swilling, scouring, eroding like a river in flood. It had no logic, no reason, no means of expression. Its energy was terrifying in its involuntary seizure, pulling my hair, banging my head on the bed. Screaming, and rushing outside, I stamped and clawed at the earth, dribbling in impotence, roaring without words. It didn't seem to be about anyone in particular. It was just a pure emotion. Until then I hadn't thought of myself as a murderous person, but at that moment I was capable of killing.

Working towards becoming forgiving began with an experience of murderous rage. In other words, I was not so totally different from the Wests as I might wish to think. I have never felt it in this way again. I was faced with the depth of the almost impossible enormity of my vow. From that moment it would not be possible to write off those people who had acted from this place. There was no room for demonising. I realised that we share a common humanity. I recognised my own capacity to inflict harm and my own need to be forgiven. Somehow this mess is something that we all face and that we cannot resolve in isolation from each other.

Later, when I thought of us all standing by Lucy's grave, the incomprehensible, unspeakable fact of the demolition of my sister and the suffering that followed in its wake, spreading its pain with the indifference and terrible destruction of an earthquake, ruptured the defence of my logic's premature compassion. My mind filled with anger and contempt. This business of forgiveness must go on hold. It almost seemed obscene: to think about forgiveness would be a betrayal of our need to grieve, to rage, to find a way forward. It was necessary to dissolve my own grief and anger and find compassion for myself before opening myself to the possibility of forgiving those who caused this terrible pain.

Over the next few years, I sat on several more silent retreats. In May 1997 I attended my fifth, again at Maenllwyd. It was here that the grief that lay beneath the murderous rage emerged. It was a turning point in my way of grieving, which had so far been private and alone. On the evening of day three an alertness began to emerge. My senses came to the fore. My body began to quicken. There was a shift from a desperate ennui of repetitive thoughts towards a feeling of casting off the trap of my mind. The sky was clear, the moon was waxing. Walking across the yard towards my bed, I saw the chestnut blossom glowing and trembling in the moonlight. My wrist dropped so that my fingers hung like chestnut leaves, limp and yielding to the movement of the air. Sleep would come easily.

However, the following day brought the next layer of suffering to the surface. My mind had been cleverly distracting me from the emotional pain that was trapped beneath its pretentious activity. My heart began to ache and my throat began to feel tight and constricted. Grief had crept up unexpectedly, as it usually does. This emotion had become familiar. A sense of panic was beginning. Where to put this feeling in the context of a Chan retreat, when all around are silent? The expression of grief can become involuntary and can develop into wailing and sometimes barking when my body needs to exorcise the horror of Lucy's death. Yet there was a commitment to stillness and silence, with nineteen other people who had made very little noise so far.

After breakfast I had an urge to run away up the valley, clawing the mud, smearing myself with it and screaming. But I asked for another interview with John (and Simon Child, who was assisting with the retreat). I said that I was fed up with grieving and that it was becoming debilitating, but that I knew that I had to go on until it wasn't sneaking up on me any more. Where was the place for me to express it within the retreat? John confirmed that it was entirely appropriate to express emotion during the meditation sessions, and to make any noises that might come up. He also said that I could go for a walk if that was what was needed.

I decided to stay with the discipline of sitting and let it happen. This was a radical decision that reflected my deep trust in John as a teacher with whom I felt safe. The tears and mucous began to pour out of my eyes and nose. Where did all that liquid come from? How many bowls would it fill? My face became wet, coated with tears and snot which dripped off my jaw. Then my whole body began to tremble and there was a heat of energy circulating and being released as my body quivered with life. My body was behaving as if it were moving towards orgasm, but the feeling wasn't sexual. It felt like a purifying fire coming up within, balancing the wetness on my face. It was as if there were a purging by fire and water.

The phrase "the vale of tears" came to mind. At first I was alone, feeling a crippling isolation. But, wading in the lake of tears, bemoaning my isolation, I was aware that it was full of others who knew this pain. There were millions of people there, all groaning, wailing and weeping: those who had undergone the Holocaust, and their remaining families; people who knew the reality of human atrocity caused by centuries of war: Bosnia, Hiroshima, Vietnam. The lake was becoming deeper. The salt water was etching more pain into our wounds. My breath exhaled with more sound. The feeling of being self-conscious and different had been dissolved. Who I thought I was, my frozen story, had somehow begun to dissolve. I was not alone.

There was nothing else to do but to remain within this massive stillness for three sessions. I felt like an ancient rock, sitting through the fluctuating seasons, years, centuries.

Later that day we were told to find a place outside in which to meditate and practise "direct contemplation". I was drawn to the ridge above the Chan Hall, to one of the sentinel Scots Pines. A huge branch had been torn away from its trunk by the wind, leaving a raw stump jutting out of its side. As I sat on the scaly branch, I was absorbed by the intense indigo of the bluebells at my feet.

As I lay back on the branch looking up at the strong trunk soaring above me, the wrenching of the branch beneath my back became real. It was then that I acknowledged the altered rhythm of the tree swaying in the soft breeze without the balance of its severed limb. At that moment there was an acceptance of the depth of my own wound. My sister has been torn out of our lives. We are all living with the severance that is left behind. At that moment there was an understanding of the reality that every violent death affects the rhythm of our shared humanity and the universe in which we are growing and dying. There was an understanding of the profound need to be gentle with my own healing and with my actions, which came from a state of woundedness. I wondered about the woundedness of the people who stole her and killed her.

That evening, John's talk "spoke to my condition", to use an old Quaker phrase. My need to understand acts of atrocity between human beings, and between humans and our shared environment, was greatly helped. He made two points that stay with me to this day. First, that evil, from a Buddhist perspective, is seen as an enormous mistake made by the perpetrator. This emphasized the need for mindfulness in all of our thoughts and actions, and the need to work towards purification and commitment to the good.

The second point was about forgiveness. John spoke about a monastery in China where the monks believe that by ringing the bells regularly at midnight they are stopping the torturers in Hell while the bells are rung. Whatever the "hell realm" may be, I felt connected with all those who are tortured by the imprisoning hell of their own minds and those who torture and are being tortured. These words gave me a glimmer of the vast compassion required to truly want to achieve this. My heartbeat quickened in response to the belief that it is a human possibility. A great sense of gratitude for these words spoken by John and an overwhelming need to thank him swept through me. As I walked slowly from the Chan Hall, the candlelight was emerging from the darkening evening air.

Chapter 8

FRESH EARTH

Inevitably, family responsibilities and the long haul of "the West case" continued. There was a struggle to balance my work as a homeopath, my contemplative time, my need to write, my family time, and my time campaigning against the making of a film about the Wests. I needed spiritual and financial support to be able to take my quest forward, and to write more. The response to *Salvaging the Sacred* was challenging my life, calling me to follow. There was more to explore, more to offer, more to be said. In the summer of 1997 I applied for a Fellowship from the Joseph Rowntree Charitable Trust. The final paragraphs of the application were:

Ultimately I would like to be able to forgive the Wests. I would hope that my journey during my year as a Fellow would help me to move in this direction, painful as it is. I need to look more deeply into the path towards forgiveness as the way to move out of the cycle of violence and abuse and to reach towards a deeper understanding of the huge love and grace involved in that realisation of our spiritual potential. By sharing this exploration in some way I would hope to be deepening the life and thought of the Society of Friends in Britain.

The response of the trustees was wise and generous. They rightly discerned that I was not in a position to do this outer work yet, as a Fellow, and could see the inner work needed more time. They had read *Salvaging the Sacred* and could see that finding the words, sharing them and the national response had changed my life. But, as one trustee said, "It's as if you are on a train that is travelling very fast and you won't know where you are until it stops." During my interview I realised that this was a deeply helpful insight. I found myself crying with relief and realised that I was actually asking for help with a way forward.

There is a proud stoicism within our family that makes asking for help difficult. An extraordinary letter arrived, offering me a grant from The Trust which would free me to take a year off work, and enable me to buy a new computer so that I could continue to explore and write about this experience. The only conditions of the grant were to find a small support group and write a report every three months. The insight, trust and generosity of this decision made a big difference to my way forward.

Six weeks before the grant period began, on 31st August 1997, the date of Princess Diana's death, I became very ill with pneumonia. During this illness I was confronted with my physical vulnerability and could no longer avoid my deep need to be still and withdraw. The message came loud and clear, "physician heal thyself". It was time to pay attention to one of the Quaker *Advices and Queries*: "Do what love requires of you, which may not be great busyness." I had to let go of my role in the world as a homeopath, and trust that stopping completely after fifteen years was going to be better for myself and for everyone else than keeping things ticking over, which is what I had hoped to be able to do. It was only after over one hundred letters to my current clients had been signed and addressed that I realised the huge amount of responsibility I had been trying to carry. The transition taught me more about the need to let go when it is time. The messages of thanks and goodwill were warming and encouraging. At last I was released to dig deeper within myself and strengthen my inner resources.

The response to *Salvaging the Sacred* required a large surface in a quiet space. I needed more time to write and to reflect. The table tennis table in the children's hut was ideal for spreading out the responses; the hut was the perfect place to write, and to meditate. So, after negotiation with my youngest son Jack, he kindly allowed me to gradually take over the hut with the understanding that he could use the pool table or the table tennis table whenever he wanted to.

The generosity and love from my children during this necessary task of grieving has affirmed that it is not necessary to hide grief away. They have also come to know more about their invisible aunt whose unique life impregnated the memories of so many others. But, in the same way that my parents' grief took them away from me, my way forward also meant a rearrangement of my time. My children's generosity, their encouragement and patience, helped me to know that they understood the importance of this journey. Yet, ultimately, like being born and dying, it is a unique, solitary endeavour which is also utterly dependent upon all forms of life.

We moved the hut further away from the house. It was now planted in a field full of bracken, by an overgrown hedge, lapped by the sound of the river and of birdsong, rising and falling with the seasons. Sometimes the chickens pecked at the polystyrene that insulated the floor. The hut became my cave, my cloister, my anchorage. The long haul through the seasons began.

Once, after a prolonged deluge, we discovered that the hut was positioned over an earlier water course. A stream was gushing along by the hedge, under the hut (which was fortunately raised up on breeze blocks) and along past the chicken house into the river. It reminded me of the water meadow in the first dream.

The space (sixteen feet by ten feet) was arranged so that two-thirds became my contemplative "sitting" area. This was mostly empty apart from my black, circular meditation cushion on a folded, antique Welsh flannel blanket that Nick had bought me with the compensation money that he received towards the cost of Lucy's coffin. He invested this money in a gift for me rather than take it as payment for his work. He is a deeply generous man.

The other third of the hut was for my desk and a selective library (poetry, theology, philosophy, Buddhist literature, holocaust literature, medieval literature, Lucy's poems and dictionaries). Sitting on the cushion felt awkward. What would arise in this space? Where was all this going?

During Rosemary West's committal trial, the pathologist had described the demolition of the bodies negatively, with the prefix *dis*. Each body, one after another (ten of them) had *dis*-articulated joints, *dis*-membered limbs. The numbing details of the number of missing bones per body, and the name of each bone that was missing, were read out for each victim. During this time of grappling, many of the words that came to mind began with *dis*. You *dis*-appeared. The effect of this, the twenty years of Not Knowing, was *dis*-abling, *dis*-connecting, *dis*-orientating, *dis*-easing. What I had thought was real was *dis*-integrating. Douglas West had also used that word. His family had *dis*-integrated upon him.

Dis- (prefix): *two ways, in twain, in different directions, apart, asunder, undo, spoil.*

Dis- is fragmenting, isolating. It keeps me from knowing and expressing the depth of my potential for good. It is separating and full of *dis*-ease. It is what I would prefer to edit out, avoid or *dis*-miss. It is what lurks inside, unresolved. It is at the root of the need to harm, the root of shame.

Harm (Old Norse: harmr) *grief, sorrow.*

How to resolve the grief and pain caused by the intention and action to harm (cause sorrow to) others? How to undo injury and harm? How to acknowledge the sorrow that you have caused (I am sorry, I take back the sorrow)? A more common response is to become more defensive, to "diss" the person harmed, to dehumanise their existence so that the pain of guilt and shame can be avoided. Many people in prison have been "dissed" and their response has been violence, a need to destroy the "disser". Prison enforces the regime of "diss".

During my first evening in the hut, after we had moved it, I was sitting in my new space feeling self-conscious, apprehensive and alone. Nick called me from the house. "There's someone on the phone." "Tell them I'm out." "No, I think you had better come." Approaching the door of the house I saw Nick standing, his hand over the receiver, mouthing "It's a Mr. West." Going into the hut was not going to be about escaping from the world out there. Whatever I was looking for was not separate from the sticky, staining mess of it all, although more solitude was important.

A deep voice with a thick Gloucestershire accent, so familiar in our rural childhood, announced that he was responding to the letter that I had sent out recently, via the Gloucestershire police, to the other families of victims. Until that moment it had not crossed my mind that other members of the West family were also in the category of "victims". Here is that letter:

As relatives of the victims we have been asked to express our views/feelings about what we wouldn't and would like to see happening on the flattened site of 25 Cromwell Street. Since March 1994 we have all been plunged into the most difficult journey that it is possible to imagine, each one of us trying to find a way to stay afloat and survive.

I was wondering if now would be the time to dare to try to talk to each other? Maybe if we could help each other to focus upon what we would like to see in the place of the source of our pain we could help each other to transform some of that suffering into a feeling of hope and moving on.

It is up to us to try to bring something positive out of the utter tragedy so that all those young lives have not been wasted. Let's try to imagine something creative and educational going on where so much suffering and cruelty occurred. It would make a big difference to each one of us, the whole community of Gloucester, and indeed the whole country. Our voices count a lot in this process. It would be a shame to lose this opportunity to bring about a change for the better.

June Gough (Lynda's mother) and I (Lucy Partington's sister) would be happy to talk with any of you who might like to phone to share your thoughts and feelings about what you would like to see happening on the site.

Please do phone either of us if you feel it would be helpful to make contact.

If you feel like writing please do. I would be glad to correspond with you. It is always helpful to share pain and work towards hope.

Sending you all good thoughts,

Douglas West, one of Fred's brothers, spoke with a voice full of confusion, shame, anger, passion and despair.

I want something at Cromwell Street that's going to show that good can come out of evil. I like the idea of a community centre. We can never obliterate what's happened but we must try to smooth out the past and make way for a better future. All you can say is that you're sorry. Fred was four years older than me. I've got three sisters and one brother.

Douglas and Fred's other brother, John, also committed suicide before his own trial, for the sexual abuse of his niece, Anne-Marie.

Douglas continued:

I live in Much Marcle. I used to see my sisters at least once a week. But the rest of the family have disintegrated on me. They all said that we shouldn't say anything to the police. But I wanted to be as helpful as I could because I want to get to the bottom of it. I want to understand why.

Fred would never defend himself in fights. We had to bale him out. I still wonder if it was the bangs on the head (he had a motorbike accident). They do say he was possibly epileptic. I've got four children aged 26, 24, 16 and 9.

It was stunning and gratifying that Douglas had found the courage to phone me. Very few people did contact us and they were not those whom I might have expected. Here was a hurt man reaching out to us who were hurt.

In the solitude of the hut, the direction of the inner work became clearer: from *dis*-member to *re*-member.

Re (prefix): *afresh, anew*

From that which is torn apart towards that which is fresh; from that which is isolated and imprisoned towards that which is joined up and free; from a self-centred sorrow towards a sorrow that dissolves into healing, knowing its place within the context of all suffering. My exploration to understand my own cycle of violence and abuse as a victim, as a perpetrator and as a bystander, to face the unresolved pain within, had hardly begun.

Lessons in winter
On black afternoons we do not see
Where the walls fold, and suck our air.
We do not see where the storm grips
The quiet voices in its urgency.

It is the same when the air
Is blurred with gold, and the trees
Caught in light –
There is nothing to understand.

The arguments have been kept too long:
Black apples, soft with frost.
We say, We cannot be deceived,
But we are afraid to touch them.

And afterwards, through eyes crammed shut,
We watch the distracting reflection, and
The mirror is blood.

We should move closer, and
Acknowledge something, it is
The love tightening in our throats makes this.
Lucy Partington

My view from the desk in my hut in the garden was an overgrown hedge. Later, the hedge was laid and the bluebells that had lain dormant secretly in the shade of the bank pushed up their green blades. Sometimes it seems to take so long to realise the consequences of choices made in the past and how they inform the present and shape the future. This process of retrospective comprehension is something to do with a relationship between remembering and meaning. The effect of these moments of insight is a physical and spiritual knowing of a truth that is beyond words. Some distant cause is realised as the trembling, unfurling bells sing a silent blue hymn of renewal.

The word "blessing" has as one of its roots the meaning of "wound" (early English "blessen": *to make sacred or holy by blood sacrifice; to mark with blood*; compare the modern French word "blessé": *wounded*). The roots of the word "innocence" mean "not harm" (Latin "nocere": *to harm*). The wound that causes sorrow can be healed by a blessing so that there is no desire to harm.

One strand of my writing and healing became to write down what occurred to me on my daily walks. From my childhood days I have known the refuge and solace of nature. Something has always been unravelling inside, keeping me open to the healing power of solitude and natural silence.

From my diary at the beginning of my grant-holder period, Autumn 1977:
Walked at 0 miles an hour up the valley curving left after the bridge, instead of right towards Graig Wen. My slow pace was partly due to weakness and partly to the slow softness of the day, full of sunshine on yellowing leaves and bracken, a slumbering, cosy pause of warmth and light before the dying begins in inexorable earnest. Arriving at the farm sooner than expected, I saw the chimney first, through the hedge of blood red rosehips. A sheepdog came barking towards me, in usual Welsh farmyard style, fierce but friendly. The farmer was standing in the doorway of a shed fiddling with something oily. He looked up and greeted me, introducing himself as Bill Ashton. He has almost white hair and a round face that expressed contentment. He began to tell me

about his life. He was one of a family of five who was born in the farm over the fields. In the 70s, one sister had died of cancer at 43, leaving five children to do a lot of fending for themselves. A brother had died in a car crash. I had never talked to Bill before and he only lives a mile away.

Talking with my neighbour Gwen Jones who is widowed and lives alone:

The dark is sometimes on us. But I always remember my mother saying to us when we were very poor and didn't have much food, "Bread can come down the chimney you know." Well that's real Santa for you isn't it? I didn't know if she meant for real that it came down the chimney. But we always had enough. Well what is enough, that's what I want to know? We always managed and that's all there is to it. That's the trouble with today. It's all about too many things. There's no room to see the glory of God. But I must stop preaching!

When I returned from my walks I used to retire to the hut to meditate, using a Chan Buddhist form of meditation called Silent Illumination. This means literally sitting as still as possible (so that "moss can grow around your mouth") and simply being with what arises in body and mind (letting through and letting be), but not elaborating upon it (letting it go). The following words, originally written in Chinese by Hung-Chih Cheng Chueh, describe what is essentially beyond words:

The clean and pure ground, wondrously bright, this is something that one has possessed from the outset. The genuine way of practice is to simply sit in stillness, and silently investigate; deep down there is a point one reaches where externally he is no longer swirled about by causes and conditions. His mind being empty, it is all-embracing; its luminosity being wondrous, it is even and impartial. Internally there are no thoughts of grasping after things; vast and removed, it stands alone in itself without any obscuration. Perfectly pure it is bright and clear.[22]

I would sometimes write about what had risen to the surface during the meditation. However, the discipline of my writing regime became less rigid as the need for time to incubate and read emerged. I was daring to push myself less and to listen to my needs with more kindness to myself.

My life was becoming simpler and quieter. It was a joy to spend more time with my family, and to clear out my cupboards. The grant had released me into more time and space. It allowed me to begin to trust and open to a simpler, more naturally joyful way of living. In the early spring I decided to participate in a three week course at Woodbrooke, a Quaker Study Centre in Birmingham. Staying in the community at Woodbrooke felt like a mixture of being back at university, being at art college and being in a monastery. It was possible to find a balance between solitude and company in an environment where Quaker values could be experienced from moment to moment.

I most valued being accepted without judgement, listened to with compassion, and being able to offer that to others. It was a joy to be taught by some of the other tutors, to be looked after by the Friends in Residence, and to meet some of the young international people who were living there and studying nearby. At the heart of life in the community at Woodbrooke are the daily silent meetings for worship. Simply "waiting on God" in shared, prayerful silence, with occasional ministry of words when one is unavoidably impelled to stand and speak.

My three weeks at Woodbrooke, participating in the Applewood module *A Staircase to Silence* felt like a speeding up of my unravelling process. I could appreciate the huge scope of the Religious Society of Friends as a structure within which I, as a unique individual, could continue my own journey towards wholeness with the support of sharing in a worshipful way with other Friends. This process of sharing my own pain and probings seemed to help others to be more open about their journeys.

One poster at Woodbrooke stays in my mind as a stern reminder: "It is better to light one candle than curse the darkness." Campaigning against the making of a film about the Wests had been draining my resources and disturbing me.

I began to let go of the need to drive myself, and returned to more nourishing family activities.

On my return from Woodbrooke I celebrated my 50th birthday by walking up Cadair Idris (our local sacred mountain). Thirty-one friends came, and we ate a picnic by the lake which is surrounded by a horseshoe of sheer cliffs, curving towards the summit. A cold wind drove some people back at this point. But twelve of us (led by my two sons) carried on into the clouds. Suddenly the sun broke through and the mists dispersed to reveal a vast view of the Welsh coast, up to the Lleyn peninsula. It felt like a real affirmation. Somehow there was enough energy to dance for a few hours in the evening.

By the spring of 1998, during my fifty-first year, I had recovered from my pneumonia, and decided to travel east for the first time to visit my daughter who was working in Nepal as part of her gap year.

Life in Nepal seemed so precarious and raw, so seemingly chaotic. Yet there, people and animals seemed to be closer to the pulse of life. There was a lack of fear and a joyful spontaneity. Was it to do with death being less hidden and denied? The proportions of life seemed more human and more spiritual. Burdens were carried in baskets on the back, slung and pivoted from the brow. Life felt closer to the rag and bone, closer to the earth.

How was it possible to feel so connected to people I had never met before, by simply gazing into their eyes and smiling? Somehow these moments emerge from a culture which invests more time in spiritual devotion and human exchange. It was more possible to "walk cheerfully over the earth answering that of God in everyone", as George Fox, who founded the Quakers in 1650, had instructed. In Nepal people greet each other with a cheerful *Namaste*, hands in prayerful respect in front of the forehead, and a slight bow, followed by a broad lingering grin, often developing into a deep laugh.

But the West invades. Coca Cola and Marlborough cigarettes wend their way up into the Himalayas on mule trains. They want what we've got. I don't want them to lose what they've got. Perhaps my travelling there adds to the loss. They gave me more than I could ever give them. They helped me to feel closer to my true nature as a human being by simply living without pretence and with an open heart. It was wonderful to be introduced to Nepalese culture by my daughter Marigold. She had been working there for three months, teaching English to the orphans living in the hostel at the Kumbeshwar technical college in Patan.

One day I visited The Golden Temple where three forms of worship were happening simultaneously every morning, beginning at 5 a.m. I meditated in the Tibetan Buddhist wing where a few monks chanted sutras, moving grains of rice from one pile to another, counting their mantras (108 *Om Mane Padme Hums*, sometimes translated as "Hail to Wisdom and Compassion", or "The Jewel in the Heart of the Lotus"). The Buddhist image of the lotus flower speaks of the transforming potential of spiritual practice in a simple but powerful way. The flower of wisdom and compassion (the jewel), is rooted in, and grows from, the mud of suffering. The repetition of mantras is one way of purifying the mud of the deluded mind that engenders its own suffering.

Women came and went offering rice and money to the monks. Other worshippers did their prostrations on the full-length board of wood, its surface shiny with the patina of devotion. In the central courtyard a gold-plated Hindu shrine was rubbed with red *tikka* paste, and showered with rice grains and marigold petals. After each offering the large bell by the entrance to the shrine was struck. This sound lifted a net of pigeons into the narrow courtyard, their flapping wings stirring the air, adding to the vigour of it all. Soon they settled back to decorate the shrine, their heads and necks bobbing down for the rice.

The courtyard was edged with Tibetan prayer wheels. Some people walked around trailing one hand along their surface as they rattled into action. The Tibetan letters shone with use, embossed and worn into a polished glow as their prayers were spun out to add to the brew in the air. Nearby, opposite the Tibetan wing, a group of men sat in a circle in another shrine room, singing Newari Buddhist devotional songs to the accompanying drum and harmonium. During my first visit they welcomed me to their circle.

This was where my Japanese friend found me. She spoke very little English but she led me, smiling and bowing to me and many of the people on her daily route, through the maze of streets, temples and courtyards to the meditation centre. Occasionally she would laugh and say "happy heart, meditation gooood!" We were given a bowl of noodles and vegetables and a cup of sweet tea by a monk in the centre. I was introduced to the Director, a Burmese Lama. He told me about the Vipassana meditation technique. Marigold had attended a ten-day, silent retreat a few weeks before I arrived, during which she had learnt this practice. We were shown into an empty hall dominated by a large statue of the Buddha. We sat in silence, side by side, meditating together. I never saw my Japanese friend again. I remember her thin, small body and her shining laugh so clearly.

As I walked back to the guest house, I saw that there was a funeral taking place by the river, on the bank below the bridge. A small group of onlookers blocked the bridge, so I took my place next to them. Somehow it felt appropriate to connect with the mourning of the death of the old man whose widow sat in a state of weak, dishevelled grief, supported by a group of women. It was the men who performed the practical details of dealing with a corpse in a hot climate. They wrapped the body with tender attention and loaded it on to a bamboo stretcher. A length of shiny cloth was laid over the top. Then the women came forward, wailing and strewing the body with flower petals.

The procession wound its way to the pyre, led by the blowing of horns. Water and oil were sprinkled onto the body by cupped hands. A circle of water was sprinkled around the funeral pyre. The fire was lit and the mourners withdrew, leaving three men to tend the cremation of the body. Later, the bones and ashes would be cast into the river. Whilst this was going on, the everyday traffic of bicycles, pedestrians, scooters and rickshaws flowed by. I felt deeply moved by the simple, elemental overtness of it all. There was nothing hidden. There was no feeling of fear. The sounds of grief were a natural, accepted expression of pain and loss. I was so grateful to have been presented with that experience. It is natural to touch and wrap a dead body. Our way in the West is not the only way.

Later, our trekking guide, who was from the Brahmin caste, told me that it is the responsibility of the eldest son to perform most of this ritual. He has to light the "wick" that is placed in the mouth of the body. He shaves his head and wears white clothing for the first year of mourning. Every year, after someone has died, there is a "death day", when the person's life is remembered. This goes on for as long as it is needed – just as in the Aboriginal culture, relatives keep a bone of the loved one until they feel able to bury it. The individual needs of the bereaved must be respected, heard and honoured. In our culture we don't leave much room for this necessary process. Our emotional health suffers accordingly. It felt affirming of the choices that I had made in relation to Lucy's bones.

The second week was spent living in a Tibetan monastery in Pokhara while Marigold and her boyfriend, Ben, were off white-water rafting. I decided not to join them. Marigold's grandmother, Nancy, who had introduced Marigold and her brother Luke to Nepal, went white-water rafting to celebrate her 70th birthday. She worked for many years with Nepali women, encouraging them and providing an outlet for their craft work in her shop "Nepal Bazaar" in Hay on Wye. She has just celebrated her 94th birthday.

I needed time for silent reflection, and to lie on the roof of the *gompa* in the humid afternoons, reading and listening to the tapes in the library, with the sounds of the semi-tropical jungle wafting around in the long rows of Tibetan prayer flags. Every late afternoon the heat exploded into a torrential thunder storm; the rain sounded like grains of rice hammering on the tin roof of my room. At night the frogs and crickets offered a spring crescendo to the strobe flashes of lightning that moved from mountain to mountain like a search light. The lake below bounced back the daily storm. It was good to simply relax into the dramatic sensuality and visual astonishment of it all.

During the third week of our holiday, Marigold and I went trekking, high in the Himalayas, with our guide, Guru Sharman. On the third day of our trek, I found myself standing in a mountain stream, in the eerie silence of the rhododendron forests, writing down these words: "As a daughter, as a mother, as a sister, as an aunt, as a niece, as a cousin, as a lover as a friend,

I totally accept my death." It felt as if the weight of my life fell away into the stream. It just didn't need to be carried any more.

The wheat harvest was in full swing, with sounds and sights of cutting the corn by sickle, carrying the sheaves back to the yards for the threshing where all ages beat out their aggression with long sticks, releasing the grain, coughing and hawking from the husks and the dust. The winnowing and sifting added a soft, whispering rhythm to the dawn air. The old people lie on thin, cane mats in the doorways, or watch the grandchildren. Many young children are left to fend for themselves all day, the older (five years old, in one case) lugging the younger ones around on their backs, tottering perilously. Our guide grew up in a rural village. He said that 40% of Nepalese children grow up or die in this way. The life expectancy of Nepalese women is fifty-two years, two years older than I was.

A few paces on, he offered me some black berries to taste. They looked like small grapes, purple with bloom. They tasted like sloes. It took me back to my earliest memory of taste – a mouth-curling sloe. This journey eastwards seemed also to be about harvesting the images of the past, from my own rural childhood that I shared with Lucy, and was now sharing with my daughter Marigold.

Two weeks after my return from Nepal, I attended another retreat with John Crook. One evening, he began his talk with the words "The mountains are doing *zazen* (sitting meditation)." I found myself suddenly crying. A memory arose of the hexagram[23] *Kên/Keeping Still/Mountain* from the *I-Ching,*[24] the ancient Chinese *Book of Changes.* The ideas in this book have played a dominant role in Chinese thinking from ancient times to the present day.

The complementary, interdependent combination of the Chinese theory of *Yin* and *Yang* is reflected in sixty-four hexagrams. *Yin* means "the shady side of the hill" and is associated with the feminine, darkness, night, earth; *yang* means "the bright side of the hill" and is associated with such words as male, sun, light, spirit of heaven. As night moves in to day so there is always a seed of *yin* within *yang,* and as day moves into night so there is always a seed of *yang* in *yin.* The light and the dark cannot exist as separate concepts.

Hexagram 52 Kên: Keeping Still, Mountain
Mountains standing close together
The image of keeping Still
Thus the superior man
Does not permit his thoughts
To go beyond his situation
In its application to man, the hexagram turns upon the
problem of achieving a quiet heart… True quiet means
keeping still when the time has come to keep still, and going
forward when the time has come to go forward. In this way
rest and movement are in agreement with the demands of
the time, and thus there is light in life.

When I had first come across this hexagram, six years after Lucy's disappearance, I was trying to decide where it would be best to root myself and the children. This hexagram seemed to answer my question. It helped me to decide to move to a Welsh farmhouse on top of a mountain looking towards Plunlumon in Penfordd Las; a place that became our home for twelve years. This place allowed me to grow closer to the nature of mountains, sitting so still with their clear curves joining the sky: sometimes coated with yellow gorse and purple heather; sometimes white with ice and snow; sometimes hidden behind horizontal rain. Always changing, yet so still, they helped me to grow closer to my true nature.

Maenllwyd and John's teachings felt close to that place. One of the lines in the words we read before meals on the retreats also expresses this feeling, a sensation that also reaches back into our childhood roaming and riding on Gretton Hill:

O silence of nature we take refuge in thee

On that same retreat, after my time in Nepal, my job was to weed the field where my tent was pitched. Uprooting the weeds, one by one, learning about their tricks and individual characteristics, became more absorbing and challenging once my resistance had released its grip. I learnt to wiggle the fork around the stones and rocks that trapped the dock roots, loosening the earth until the broad, green leaves moved up towards me, followed by their single or double thick, yellow roots that had the look of mandrakes. It became satisfying to track the deepest tips of these stubborn plants, digging out stones and wiggling the fork in deeper. Getting to the bottom of it, pulling it out in one go, after careful loosening. It would never grow again.

Of course there were the devious illusions, with their leaves full of stinging hairs, and their roots spreading far from their leaves, like the nettles. Tackling them with my gloved hands, I still managed to be stung. They would grow back in time, as their root systems are more difficult to trace and remove. They require patient, long term investigation and gradual removal. As for the thistles, they didn't fool me for long. It was a matter of a firm grip and a sharp pull. Up came the white, short, single root. They won't come back, unless the odd one escapes to flower and spread its downy seeds.

I was aware of this process going on in my mind in relation to my inherited *karma*.[25] Maybe it is possible to create the space for a meadow full of flowers.

Chapter 9

SUFFERING AND HEALING

It was in late winter 1999, five years after Lucy's remains were found, that I had had the fifth and most challenging of my dreams. It included a premature decision to forgive Rosemary West, but the figure of Rosemary represented far more than West's wife. Significantly, the dream was in two parts.

We met on the edge of a park, by some railings with spiked ends. It was night, and dark, apart from the greyish orange of street lights giving the sky a sleazy glow. We faced each other and I said (without looking at her face), "I forgive you." The words came out limp and monotonous as the litter that blocked the drain near my foot. It was a meaningless moment of misguided, arrogant hypocrisy. There was no response. She evaporated into the drain. The railings were spears of ice. The skin on my hands froze and tore as I tried to loosen my grip. How could I have been so patronising and pretentious, so premature? Forgiveness, what does it mean and how will it come?

In the next scene of the same dream I was sitting in a basement with Rosemary West and another woman who said that she was a mediator. Rosemary was scooping handfuls of flesh from a glistening pile of meat, as bloody and fresh as chopped placentas, on the floor by her feet. She was pushing them into small, polythene bags. She lined up the bags. They looked like chicken giblets from the innards of frozen, supermarket poultry. On the wall behind her there was a dark space, like a window with no glass in it, opening onto a blackout night sky. She picked up each bag in turn, tossing them one by one over her shoulder into the black rectangular frame. She didn't turn her head to follow her actions once. Her eyes were all pupil that strained towards me like a sharp point trying to burst through a bin liner. She repeated a sentence to herself; the tone was matter of fact, like a chant without heart: "I keep throwing them into the sea, but the waves keep bringing them back."

I looked at the mediator with triumphant illogic. Rose must be mad if she thinks that the sea is outside the basement. How can I speak to someone who is so mad as to think that the sea is outside the basement? It is not possible to understand or relate to anyone who is so mad as to think that the sea is outside the basement. My sense of reality has nothing in common with hers. "I keep throwing them into the sea, but the waves keep bringing them back."

She could not see us. Her face was white and cold as china clay. She had no fire left. Her fingers clawed and stuffed, clawed and stuffed. The bags of flesh, purple, putrid, went over her shoulder, into the hole, one after another. But as I looked closer, sure enough, the number of bags was simply increasing. The words guttered on:

"I keep throwing them into the sea, but the waves keep bringing them back."

The mediator had gone. I didn't see her leave. My focus was drawn towards the power of the sea. I couldn't hear it, but it wasn't swallowing those bags of flesh. The sea knows the rules. It would not absorb or accommodate the rotting flesh. It would not allow it to disappear. There was nowhere for it to hide. Soon the room would be full of these neat, transparent bags that refused to follow the rules of waste disposal. Rose was intoning a universal law. The words didn't seem to touch her, but they came out of her mouth:

"I keep throwing them into the sea, but the waves keep bringing them back."

Here was the need to face more of the easily demonised "Rosemary West" in me, my own shame and guilt and the bits

I would rather edit out. Rosemary West could not rid herself of the contents of the basement in Cromwell Road (which she continues to deny knowing anything about). I would rather edit out my "terminations".

The metaphors of this dream were hard to face and bear, but I understood that they were a necessary step in facing the next layer of the darkness of denial within.

Towards the end of another retreat, after five days of "sitting very still", I re-connected with every person that "arose" within me and asked for forgiveness, for all of the failed moments (when I was not fully there). This was painful: there seemed to be endless moments like this. I also realised that maybe I had rarely been fully present and this led to a wave of grief and regret about my wasted life. Learning to be more compassionate to myself is difficult but essential to my well-being and that of people with whom I come in contact.

Gradually, as I continued to work through the layers, through writing and contemplation, a thick sorrow was identified and felt, sticky with decades of avoidance, throbbing relentlessly within my rib cage, clotted and fixed. It was a longing, a yearning, a disharmony that quickened into a beating fear, like a small child with its fists on a door that won't open. Where is the sanctuary in the face of impermanence, in the face of death? Who am I really? That question wouldn't leave me alone. It called me away from all that was supposed to keep me "on track" and "secure". My home, my husband, my family, my work, could not give me the place that was sought. There was nothing to hold on to in the world out there. It is always changing. No matter how hard I tried, it could not be controlled so that I felt safe.

It was time to investigate this sorrow because it wouldn't go away. Blaming other people for its existence was neither beneficial nor releasing. All those gestures and words that kept me firmly intact behind this mask of "coping" and being "all right" needed to drop away. Conforming to what society expects is to be not authentic. Everything must go when I am alone with my death, my passing from this world to another. Can this other world be revealed through the death of "I" before I die? Is it necessary to search?

Is this thick sorrow a broken heart? It certainly aches and brings forth tears. Are they tears of self pity? It is so easy to cry. Everything seems so sad. It is as if there is no real meaning, just a perpetual cycle of stabs in the dark, that make more stabs in the dark. But thinking about it, trying to describe it, trying to understand it, is also a distraction, a vain attempt to keep its power at bay. But whatever it is needs to be allowed to come to me. I can go no further on my own. It is a place that is full of death, loss, and skulls. It is a place of tidal waves, earthquakes, and hurricanes. It is a deep, spiritual crisis.

It is not just about the loss of Lucy: it is also a deep regret that my life has not been well used. It is a fear of all the dead people that I have tried to be, that I have failed to be, that I no longer want to be. It is a fear of too much yearning to belong in some way, to be valued, to be worthy, to be fulfilled before I die. But "I" needs to die, as the fourteenth-century Dreamer had to learn. It's also a feeling of having so much to give, a yearning to give but nowhere to put it.

Always there is a core of sadness at the heart of me. It is deeply unsatisfactory, like a thickened trunk of ivy, constricting the tree of my life, slowly killing it. There is a fear that if the python-ivy is severed the tree will keel over. It is like a tourniquet, stopping the flow of arterial blood from a deep wound. There is a fear that if the tourniquet is untwisted the blood will gush forth, draining out into death. The wound must be unwrapped, kindly, in case it starts to bleed again. If it isn't unwrapped my gait will be altered by the loss of a limb. Who is truly waiting to be known without "I" will not be born.

This feeling originated in my adolescence. It was as if I were going bad inside, strangely stagnant and discarded, disconnected from love. It is about general loss, an inexorable loss that sees through the delusion of all that I have tried to shore up into some kind of identity. This grasping for recognition, for attention, for love has been at the centre of my world. When I look at it all like this for so long, it seems almost impossible to change my habits, to untwist it all, to erase the rat runs of my mind.

It is called the "human condition", this desire for life to be happy and secure, pleasurable, free from pain. It's what we all desire. Grasping and greedy, consuming and hoarding, we slam the door shut. We bolt it against thieves and murderers. Hating, we push away, trying to destroy anything or anyone who threatens this precarious, deluded state of self-important existence. We are ignoring the reality that none of these attitudes and actions can change the fact that life is uncertain and always changing and that we are "all in this together" and that bolting in or bolting out deepens the pain. But this time it must be faced and accepted. This time it feels as if this is the only way to proceed.

There are three major traumas that could be blamed for this thick sorrow of mine – three reasons at the root of the stemmed gash. They all happened and they all made a wound; that much is true. They are all about the betrayal of love, the betrayal of trust, the betrayal of innocence. They all led to a weakening of confidence, a deep confusion, and a need to find some sort of security again. The actions that came from this wounding made more wounds.

The first two (the effect upon me of our parents' divorce when I was twelve years old, and Lucy's disappearance when I was twenty-six) led to a shameful cycle of betraying others, of losing trust in life and relationships. The third (finding out about the unimaginable atrocity of Lucy's death when I was forty-six years old) led to the place that confronts me now. But the imprint of all three is interconnected beyond time and memory. Then there were the actions of those who betrayed me, which came from their experience of being betrayed, so there is no beginning really, just unresolved pain, going back through aeons. This view is turgid, brutal and shameful; deceitful, treacherous and pitiful.

What has been locked in, or locked out? There are many words but they all fail. Why has it taken so long to face the painful truth of my life, to open my arms to it before it has gone? There is everything to lose, but it is time to find something new, or discover what lies beyond this endless cycle of violence and revenge, to transform this shrivelling, mean attitude of self-made suffering. These old, outlived positions, postures, attitudes need to die once and for all. It is time to learn the deepest lesson that faces us all, to aspire towards a more spacious, generous and wise way of being human.

Between Lucy's disappearance and her discovery, Not Knowing was about a violation of continuity, an extreme experience of the reality of impermanence. Such experience threatens one's ability to find truth, but also offers a chance to look again: to move to a Knowing of a kind different from that of 1994. The truth that went before is separated from me by a chasm, a gaping hollow. How to join up the life before with the life that is rent apart? How to integrate the reality of violent loss? How to transform a gap into a space that is free of pain: the healing, the opening?

Lucy's priest said "grace is with us all the time". This is another "barnacled word", grace. Maybe it is a feeling of being upheld and guided in some way, when you are called to do what is required but you can't explain it, when you are "out of the way" and living for others. It could be used to describe the moments in the mortuary when we were honouring and wrapping Lucy's bones. It involves a feeling of lightness and gratitude. Sometimes it is a moment of insight, a glimpse of comprehending what is in the way of that which is ultimately beyond comprehension. So why do some people lose touch with it, as I had done, as the Wests did, as we all do? To use an old Quaker phrase, how do we learn to "walk in the light?" This journey would not have happened and continue to happen without grace. How do we create the conditions in which it can be known and flourish?

The Buddhist retreats offered a new way of practice and a fresh understanding of these barnacled words. The intensive, rigorous training operated within a carefully structured discipline of prolonged silence, meditation practice, private interviews with the teacher, Buddhist teachings and work periods. All provided a safe, uninterrupted space in which to stay true to what was arising within me and investigate it. This exacting spiritual practice offered an ancient lineage of Chan training to the lineage of suffering in our family, a means to transform a frozen story and bring us into a world closer to our "kynde", our human flourishing.

In July 2000, Master Sheng Yen came to the UK to lead another retreat. By the fourth day I was struggling and could feel this horrible depression. It felt as if I didn't want to go on breathing. It was too much effort. It all started to surface again. "Oh no, I thought I had finished with all this. The self I have had enough of is this snivelling, grieving mess."

Maybe this feeling came from the exhaustion and obstruction of refusing to let go of my quest and the need for this attitude to change in some way. Maybe I was fabricating this place of isolation and lack of hope; an obstinate state of self-pity; anger gone wrong, stagnant, with no outlet. It was a feeling that nobody cared who I was. As the parcel of flesh had been thrown out of the window, the sea had brought it back and there was no energy left to throw it out again, and no interest in repeating that mistake, in going on in that way. Maybe it was *acedia* (sloth): a strange stupor, a torpor, a stuck numbness, a worn-out grief. It felt as if it was too much effort to go on breathing.

I found myself in my only interview with the great Chan master (with five other people) blurting out that I was struggling with a deep karmic obstruction and that I was also feeling that I didn't want to go on breathing. John Crook added the information that my sister had been murdered. Neither Shifu nor his attendant monk, Guo Yuan Fa Shi (the Abbot from Dharma Retreat Centre in Pine Bush, New York), looked at me. They spoke rapidly in Chinese and then the Abbot gave me an interpretation. I realised that my whole life (and maybe previous lives) had led to this point.

When this state was laid bare before Master Sheng Yen my great fortune was revealed. This ripening of pain could be offered and shared. My life had converged on this moment, this privileged moment with a monk (as he humbly described himself) who has devoted nearly the whole of his life to the Buddhist pursuit of wisdom and compassion in order to be able to help others move that way too. He said that Lucy's death and my present grief were *for the benefit of all living beings.*

He then said, softly and simply:

> *Just know that your suffering is relieving*
> *the suffering of others.*

I thought of Jesus dying for our sins and *Tonglen* (the Tibetan Buddhist practice of breathing in the suffering of others and breathing out compassion). I asked him if he meant that I should pray (in my experience, a good method for transforming one's own pain into the desire for the well-being of others), or practise *Tonglen*. But he said no.

> *Just know that your suffering is relieving*
> *the suffering of others.*

Does this mean that there is a possibility of a steadfast attitude within me that is helpful to others if I simply stay true to my own suffering through self-investigation and an openness to that which arises? Does it mean that by continuing to face the unresolved pain as it arises, accepting it and letting it go, without getting attached to it or pushing it away, without elaborating on it or dwelling on it, I will have more insights, more seeing through the delusions created by the mind?

This approach involves not trying to bypass suffering (self-avoidance, denial). Denial is an important part of survival, but as a conclusive position it is an attempt to avoid, trivialise and negate or delay the pain of the healing process, to fix it and make it more comfortable to live with. Denial can lead to lethal, oppressive regimes. I have tried that one, and sometimes wish that it would work for me, but it left me in a frozen silence which is driven by a wish to deny pain, and it carries a perverse power which can haunt, oppress and sometimes destroy vitality.

It also involves not allowing the suffering to destroy me (self–blame, suicide). It is hugely difficult to allow and "enfold" the dark pain whilst not being overwhelmed and corrupted by it. This feeling of inexorable despair, and helplessness that this is never going to go away (be resolved) consumes the hope of change. There seems to be no energy to move. This is another aspect of the frozen silence.

It involves not dumping the pain on others (arrogance, blame, murder). This attitude drives the cycle of violence and abuse. Murderous rage is terrifying in its almost involuntary power. The ignorance of demonising an "other" and denying any sense of personal responsibility lies at the heart of vengeful, violent actions.

This attitude of insight and compassion, that is able to love my enemies and pray for them, is waiting to be known and expressed beyond that which is "right" or "wrong". If only "I" (my small self that I cling onto as my only identity) can get out of the way. To be able to live from a place of profound interconnection, from "the peace that passeth understanding", to be genuinely liberated from all negative, afflictive emotions, to experience the reality of non-duality and the universal nature of being alive, offers the most creative, positive way forward.

Yes, it must involve giving up all hope of a better past and is the kind of full-stop that offers a new relationship with the present moment, with all that is arising now. This is about cultivating circles of compassion (empathy with suffering). It is also the territory of true justice (that which enables a lack of prejudice, an understanding, a grace of being). It is that which takes us out of our small self into the larger self of the whole universe, where we realise that who we are is truly interconnected. Here we become naturally well-wishing to all forms of life. In this place forgiveness is spontaneous.

My initial motive for beginning this journey was for the sake of my children. I had realised, in terrible depth, the reality of the cycle of violence and abuse: we pass on our unresolved pain to the next generation. I have been trying to explore my feelings and integrate the dreadful reality of Lucy's death in a way that does not pass on my struggle with anger, bitterness and grief as well as the aftermath of a difficult trial and media coverage. I have needed to know how I could use my life to stop this cycle of violence, abuse and revenge, without denying the devastating effect that it has had upon us all.

> *Just know that your suffering is relieving*
> *the suffering of others.*

Not until much later did I learn that this "offering up" of pain for universal benefit is a common Catholic practice. Could Lucy have been able to "offer up" her torture? If she was able, what an unimaginable abundance of grace did she release into the world!

After the interview with Master Sheng Yen I returned to sit very still. Back on my cushion, the grief flooded back, and my desire to breathe returned. I thought of Rosemary West. She was fifteen years old when she was abducted from a bus stop and raped. Her pleas (one can presume?) were not answered during the years of sexual abuse that she suffered from her father and her brother. Her moral lens was utterly distorted ("dissed") and her traumatised, toxic patterns attracted another violent abuser, her future husband, Frederick West. She was nineteen years old when Lucy (who was twenty-one years old) was gagged into anonymity, raped, tortured and killed or left to die.

In my mind I tried to say to Rosemary, half-heartedly, reluctantly, sceptically, "I am feeling a terrible pain that won't go away, but I hope that it might help you in some way." Then the most profound realisation of the depth and extent of the suffering that she has created for herself and many others was revealed.

In that moment my heart was awakened. There was a felt, embodied saturation of comprehending. There was a moment of insight into the complex cage of the fear, rage, shame, guilt and unresolved grief of her mind. Then there was the connection with the reality of this life-long imprisonment, of being locked away and demonised in a society that hates her, and with how, perhaps irrevocably, her family is wrecked and fragmented. There was a searing feeling of her isolation and shame. In that moment, my own deepest shame surfaced again and was faced, the unborn children "terminated" during the early years of Not Knowing when my life was also confused, isolated and unresolved.

> I keep throwing them into the sea,
> but the waves keep bringing them back.

In that moment of unexpected, authentic compassion for Rosemary West, my pain went away. It had changed from "I am feeling this *because* of you (blame)" to this feeling is *for* you, that you may be free. This was a well-wishing with no expectation of response or reward, an expression with less of the small self.

The word "forgiving" became alive. The aeons of barnacles of impossible piety that have encrusted the possible experience signified by this word "forgiveness" with religious, pretentious dogma just dropped away: *for*-giving. The bars of thick sorrow dissolved – or at least a new relationship with pain was formed, because it is *for* someone else in order that they may be free of that which caused them to harm in the first place – giving for, *for*-giving. The unexpected by-product of this compassion (empathy with suffering) seems to be a feeling of being freed, being more alive, released in some way.

> *Love bade me welcome: yet my soul drew back,*
> *Guilty of dust and sin.*
> *But quick-eyed Love, observing me grow slack*
> *From my first entrance in,*
> *Drew nearer to me, sweetly questioning,*
> *If I lacked anything.*
>
> *A guest, I answered, worthy to be here:*
> *Love said, You shall be he.*
> *I the unkind, ungrateful? Ah my dear,*
> *I cannot look on thee.*
> *Love took my hand, and smiling did reply,*
> *Who made the eyes but I?*
>
> *Truth Lord, but I have marred them: let my shame*
> *Go where it doth deserve.*
> *And know you not, says Love, who bore the blame?*
> *My dear, then I will serve.*
> *You must sit down, says Love, and taste my meat:*
> *So I did sit and eat.*[26]
> **George Herbert**

A disc of warm, bright light fills my chest, spreading with confidence, pushing the sad voice, the self-centred story out through my throat. The circling buzzards, the tumbling ravens, the glistening cobwebs, the scarlet rowan berries, the endless, blue sky enter. Here is an inner sanctuary, throbbing away with gentle assurance. It feels pure and lasting, receiving and giving, breathing in, breathing out. It is the joyful mystery of being alive, beyond human comprehension. If we are all part of each other, even beyond our physical "passing", our breathing out for the last time from this body, then to withhold compassion towards any form of life lessens our true place of belonging and destroys our potential community.

Learning to face what needs to be healed within me as I turn (re-pent) towards the greater whole, towards that which is pure, was a step towards the dissolving of my little self.

All – almost all – who have been touched by Lucy's life, her disappearance and her terrible death have been enlarged in some way, have known a deepening of love. This is truly more enduring than the horror surrounding the unspeakable physical trauma. It is as mysterious as the dreams that guided me and the words that arrived. It is embodied in the root of her name, Lucy.

> lux, lumen, lucere (Latin): *light, to shine*
> leuk (Aryan root): *to shine, be white*
> leuhto (Old Norse): *that which is bright*

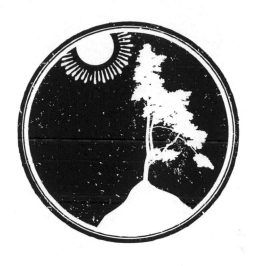

Transforming

Chapter 10

LUCY'S WOVEN BAG

There is a field on Gretton Hill called the Top Ground, where we kept our pony, Felix. One day, when Lucy was nine years old, she walked around the edge of the field gathering raw sheep's wool from the hedges. Then she carried it back to our home, The Mill, and carefully transformed it into a little woven bag.

The whole process must have taken days of intense concentration, patience and a determination to follow an idea through in practice. It speaks of her gentleness and her generosity, and her desire to get back to first principles.

Lucy gave the bag to me. It is one of my most treasured possessions; it used to contain my embroidery silks, now it holds my prayer beads. As I remember her making it, painstakingly, with patience and determination, it struck me that this process was another clue, a thread that it has taken me so long to follow. As well as telling us a great deal about Lucy's nature and her methods of making, the little bag's creation seems to re-echo the pattern of *Pearl* which has informed this whole book.

This initial, messy *crisis* relates to the beginnings of Lucy's bag. She pulled the raw fleece from the barbs of brambles, fences and hedgerows. This matted, raw fleece was choked with thorns, twigs, moss, earth and dried sheep shit. This speaks of the thick sorrow that can seem too complex to tease out.

Back at The Mill, Lucy faced the raw fleece. Her creative inspiration led her to carefully snap large thorns away from the branches of a rose bush and push them through two sheets of cardboard. These were the carders needed to loosen and clean the sheep's wool. She used thorns to extract the thorns, slowly untangling the knots and clots as the dirt dropped away. The thorns of unresolved pain in the mess of the wool were released by the thorns of confessing. Patiently she worked through the grubby pile until she produced a mound of soft, untangled wool: her professing.

The third stage of making the bag was the spinning of the thread. Lucy took a cotton reel and a pencil to make her spindle. Lifting soft clumps of carded fleece, her fingers twisted it into the beginning of the thread, somehow attaching it to the end of the pencil and the cotton reel spindle. This was twiddled and dropped, allowing the weight and turning of the spindle to twist the fleece into a long thread which she wrapped around the pencil. The thread is uneven, sometimes thick and then thinner but unbroken and long. This is the thread of comprehending, a new, strong line to follow and weave.

Finally, Lucy made a loom from a rectangular frame of sticks tied together. First she made the warp stretching the thread from one end of the frame to the other then she wove the weft from side to side, over and under, creating a length of woollen cloth. She carefully bound the ends after removing the sticks. Folding the cloth into thirds, she sewed up the sides for four inches, leaving a flap of four inches that tucks over the opening. It is four inches square. She had separated out some dark-brown fleece and used this to weave two thin stripes which lie under the flap of the bag near the top. The raw wool was transformed. She chose to give it to me. Over forty years later it would be shared with others and would bring about astonishing moments of transformation. Its gentle, hand-made warmth would travel with me into the dark pain of prisons.

In 2001, a year after the retreat with Chan Master Sheng Yen, my inner journey began to ripen unexpectedly into a new form. I was invited to spend a day at Her Majesty's Prison Grendon and Springhill, one of the UK's three therapeutic prisons. Part of the regime is to offer Visitors' Days which are hosted by the prisoners.

I found myself sitting next to a tall, broad man in his early thirties, wearing a white nylon shirt, who asked, "Do you know what the theme is today?" I replied, "No, I didn't realise that you had themes." "It's victims. And when we were looking through the list of visitors we were told that one of them is the sister of a West victim." "That's me", I disclosed in a matter of fact way. His response was immediate and authentic. He showed curiosity and concern, which was shushed by the beginning of the presentations. He offered me a peppermint and whispered that he was on soon, and implored me to give him "some eye contact. I'm dead scared." I felt strangely maternal, nodding with encouragement.

He began to speak, tearfully, discarding his written speech that he must have sweated over. "My name is Angus and I'm serving eight years for armed robbery. I entered the bank and held up a customer at gunpoint. I held her from behind in a neck hold and put the gun to her head." Silence. I suck the peppermint and catch his eye. "There isn't a day goes by when I don't think about her. There isn't a day goes by when I don't think about Anne. I wonder how her life is now. I wonder if she had to give up her job because of my crime. I wish I could know. I wish I could tell her how bad I feel about what I did. I wish she could know that." He breaks off and says that's enough. Then he's sitting next to me. I pat his shoulder. His forearms and his huge hands agitate. So this is an armed robber. Why don't I feel threatened by him, now that I know the violence of his crime? Our first contact was direct and empathic, no room for prejudice. I hope we can keep it that way. It would be easy to slip into fear or fantasy.

The next person to speak was the Governor of Grendon, Tim Newell. He spoke about the "culture of enquiry" that underpins the Grendon approach. This phrase stuck in my mind. I felt privileged to be part of a community of seekers for a day. We divided into different wings and left the hall, walking past football pitches and raised flowerbeds, until our small group entered D wing.

The smell of school dinners and the sound of loud rap music came from the kitchens. I learnt that part of the therapeutic regime is for the prisoners to take responsibility for their cooking and cleaning. We would all be eating together later. I didn't see any prison staff around. We were shown into a room with a circle of chairs. We were offered a coffee. A few tablespoons of instant coffee granules sagged in the corner of a polythene bag, next to scattered tea bags and some dried milk. The stainless steel jug of hot water was getting cooler, and no-one seemed to be serving, so we began to help ourselves. The tension was increasing. We sat in the circle. Six prisoners and six visitors. No-one else. This was "any questions" time. Tom was the facilitator in our group. He suggested that we went around the circle saying why we were there.

He began. His name, his age, the time he was serving, his crime: rape. He was in his early thirties.

I was the first visitor to speak.

My name is Marian and I'm here because my sister, Lucy, was a victim of violent crime. I have been searching for some sort of truth and understanding about my sister's brutal death. Like all of you in Grendon, I have ended up having to search inside myself, investigating my own cycle of violence and abuse. I have found debilitating grief, fear, shame and murderous rage. I would like to be able to understand what kind of circumstances lead to the acting out of these impulses that we all seem to have within us. Lucy was gagged when she died. That is one of the most difficult aspects of her death for me. She couldn't speak her truth. I would like to listen to you.

How would we continue? Tom took the lead. He turned to look me in the eye. "What you said has really affected me. Until I heard you speaking like that, I think I had just been playing at victim empathy. Something has hit home." A moment of contact and impact that leaves both of us exposed and vulnerable. For me it goes something like this. In my gut (rather than my head where I had already worked it out) I am struck by the realisation that by sharing something of my experience of Lucy's death with men who have committed violent crimes I help them to experience victim empathy, which may in turn help them not to re-offend and to integrate their own victim pathology.

This experience in Grendon prison prepared me for the next step. Tim Newell invited me into the world of restorative justice. This approach to justice sees crime as harm done that needs healing for all those who have been affected. The power of the process lies in the fact that it offers a place for the *dis-* to be expressed and heard and for movement towards the *re-*. It offers a space for the action of grace.

It involves the expression and acknowledgement of that which has been lost (not simply on a factual, material level), the context of the crime (what was going on in the personal lives of all of the people involved in the crime), the experience of empathy, the feeling of remorse, the offering of apology, the understanding and maybe the offering of forgiveness. It was as if my inner search had led to an outer form.

I began going into prisons on a regular basis, sharing "our" story with the inmates. Two weeks after a visit to Horfield Prison, I received a letter from one of the prisoners.

Dear Marian,

I would like to say thank you for coming to Horfield prison to talk to us about how victims of crime feel. It made me look deep into my heart about the effect my drug problem was having on people, mostly the victims.

I used to look upon the houses I broke into as just another house. But your visit opened my eyes. I started putting faces to my crimes which had a big impact on me. Women and children, I had taken away their sense of security. Plus little things that seem worthless to me might mean the world to the victims.

I contacted the police. They took me out today to my flat in Bristol where I showed them stolen items and little things that might mean a lot to my victims. I gathered all the things together then asked them to take me out in the car where I showed them the houses I burgled, so the property could be returned. I shocked myself by doing this because the police could not prove beforehand that it was stolen. I'm in a bit more trouble now but it's worth it to know some people have got their things back. I told the police to say I was sorry. I know it will not change a lot. But it's a big change for me. Thank you. Yours Paul

I've put a poem with this letter. I hope you like it:

> **End to beginning** *(excerpt)*
> *Morning dew to evening sun*
> *Winter days to summer trees*
> *Withered plants to honey bees*
> *Old to new*
>
> *Broken lives to unfulfilled dreams*
> *Deserted lands to glaciers of snow*
> *Light of truth*
> *Sands of time start to flow*
>
> *Faded promises, distant dreams*
> *Darkened soul becomes*
> *Heart so bright*
> *Time to forgive, the broken*
> *Child begins to fight.*

Paul then wrote again:

> *Thank you for writing back to me. I've been on C Wing two weeks now after completing the F Wing course. I've managed to stay clean from all drugs. I've been searching all my life to feel good about myself and not feel like a reject of society. I'm starting to love myself and others around me. I've spent many years hating and resenting others for my downfall. My heart was like a furnace. I'm not sure what made me who I am (poem enclosed).*

> **Innocent** *(excerpt)*
> *I wish to fly away from*
> *My wicked ways*
> *To find light of strength*
> *To undo what I have*

Sowed, to find the sweet
Taste of brighter days.

I might not be responsible for being down. But I am responsible for getting up! I am so grateful for what you and the team of people have done for me. You have not just made me realise what impact and harm I do to my victims, but what harm and destruction I do to myself as well.

I hope I get the chance to say sorry to my victims. I thought the other night about the way I affected them, the way they must be feeling. I feel so helpless, I just want to put things right.

I just hope and pray that one day restorative justice will be introduced into all prisons. Without this what chance do people have of breaking the chain?

Letter 5:
Now I look back on my life I can see I was put in a prison of my own when I was a child and that place is a lot more lonely and devastating. At least I can hear the birds sing here and through my window feel the sun on my face. That childhood prison was cold and pitch black.

I know what it is like to feel confused and not know what you are supposed to be doing. I thought I would write a poem to cheer you up and I hope you like it.

Time to heal
A time to heal, a time to dance and be free
Forgiveness for every soul
We hold the key

The sundial and peace inside
We all need
Anger and resentments will never succeed
Solitude – heights of the mountains
The loneliness of the desert
Time to reflect
Let all your pain go
As you bathe in the gracious blue fountains
The void within the soul

The gardens of peace we can feed
The lushes of yellow and green flowers
From seeds to beauty
We watch them grow

The sound of the rivers
Rushing waters to a steady flow
In all this beauty will we find
To hear the sweet songs
From the singing birds

The heart and soul becomes combined
The flowers , the roses row in row
We are no different
We are how they grow

The light, the rain, the sun
Is what they have
We have all this and more
So why be sad?

I'd never written a poem in my life before I met you. And the only way I can let go of the pain and express myself – speak from the heart – is poetry.

I never knew Lucy used to write poems. I would like to dedicate all my poems to Lucy because in a strange way if it wasn't for what happened to her we would never have met and I would still be in that dark lonely place.

Every time I write or read one of my poems I will remember how you and Lucy pulled me from the dark lonely pit which would have destroyed me.

Letter 8:
I did receive the book of Lucy's poems from your mam. It was a wonderful read. I can say it was fuel to my fire. The poem Sea Horses *was beautiful, it brought a tear to my eye. Thanks for sharing them with me.*

Sea Horses

I was walking across the bleak, grey moor
On a cold and lonely night;
When a silvery mist began to form
And blot out the evening light.

Thicker and thicker it swirled about me,
So dense I could hardly see
I stood there, lonely, frightened and lost
There was nobody, nobody there, but me.

Suddenly I heard a faint, far sound
Muffled by the thickening fog;
The sound of galloping horses' hoofs!
I stood transfixed on the edge of a bog.

Nearer and nearer I heard them come,
Until they galloped quickly past me
A herd of glistening white sea horses,
Galloping up from the sea!

Then it was all over, they were gone
Beautiful, wild and gay -
The mist had lifted, and I slowly
Walked my homeward way.

Many a night since I have walked up there,
In rain and fine, but never a gleam
Of white sea horse was ever there -
It must have been all a beautiful dream!
Lucy Partington

Paul continued:

I don't think people realise the impact that a few words can bring. Words can be very powerful. ......Negative, positive they can have a BIG impact on our lives. The day I found the hope that was stolen from me was the day I met you in HMP Bristol. You spoke and looked at me as if I was a human being. It was like a seed that was planted inside me. All the parts that were ripped from me in my past started to grow again...

During my work as a homeopath, I listen to stories of pain that need healing. In my prison work, I found myself in the same role.

On another visitors' day at Grendon Prison I sat opposite a large tattooed man at lunchtime. He told me that he was in prison because he had murdered his wife when he was drunk. Eighty percent of crime is fuelled by drugs and alcohol. Both reduce the ability to take responsibility for one's life in an attempt to escape from the reality of pain and death. This is known as "self-medication". Keeping oneself away from knowing oneself.

We looked at each other in silence for a while. My response was silent tears. He has to live with the trauma of that moment of alcohol-fuelled rage, expressed as fatal violence. He killed his wife, now he was missing her. He nodded and continued to eat his lunch. What else was there to say?

> *Love, accept my rich sighs,*
> *They are nobody else's:*
> *Spontaneous gold.*
>
> *My relations are dying;*
> *The vigils I keep will*
> *Worry me to death.*
>
> *Flowers I kill scrupulously,*
> *Wearing my old shoes-*
> *Observe them.*
>
> *Love, note my fallenness-*
> *A subtle sacrament;*
> *I do no thing perfectly.*
>
> *I can forgive too*
> *Forgiveness? I can forgive too.*
> *Why won't you be forgiven?*
> **Lucy Partington**

It concerns me that in our culture, we seem to have forgotten about the part of the journey that moves from revenge towards becoming more *for*-giving.

The desire for revenge is a common reaction to traumatic loss. It is deeply corrosive.

I corresponded with Fergal Keane on this subject. In November 2000, Keane wrote an article for *The Independent* entitled *How our country made two children into killers.*

He had written:

There is nothing in my world so terrifying as the thought that harm will be wrought on my child, and nothing so sure as my sense that **the hope for vengeance** would live with me **for ever.**

I wrote to him, in response to his article, asking:

Do you envisage direct action, divine vengeance or simply a general mode of continuing anger and bitterness, for ever? Or do you imagine that you would never be able to be free of it? Or do you imagine that you would want that as a reason to go on living? Could you elaborate on what you mean?

I can only say that I have committed myself to **the hope for forgiveness** and that if you found yourself in the position that you have dared to imagine I feel sure that you would not want to remain stuck for ever in the prison of desire for vengeance. After a while, you may realise the excruciating truth of a Chinese saying: "He who cannot forgive must dig two graves."

He replied:

Thanks once again for your letter. I don't think I have read anything that has moved me so much in a long time. But it has also challenged me profoundly. I know that when I wrote about feeling sure of my hope of vengeance I was being as honest as I could about what I believed my reaction would be. Would that rage endure forever?

Of course you are right. How can I confidently predict that my feelings would last forever? Would it be the "right" feeling to have?

I don't think feelings are right or wrong – they simply are; it is a question of how/whether we act on our feelings. The more useful question, and the question that goes to the heart of the matter, is whether such a feeling, especially as an enduring force in one's life, is good for me, for those that I love and for humanity as a whole.

The answer is of course as you have described: no, it would be deeply unhealthy on a personal level, and in terms of broader humanity, to cling to the wish for vengeance. I have tried in my own life to set the past, if not quite behind me, at least in a place where it no longer has the power to distort my life and my relationships. The pain and emotional abuse suffered in an alcoholic home were indeed sources of bitterness; for years I sank into the world of alcoholism myself, too often using the past as a justification for my actions. A few years back I was confronted with a choice: to die from a disease that had killed my father, or to try and stop the cycle, to save my own life and do everything I could from passing on the unhappiness to my own child.

A huge part of the process has been acceptance, recognising that my father was not a bad man. I have learned to accept him and love him. My only sorrow is that this process happened after he died. But acceptance has liberated me in a way that I find hard to convey. It is a gift I give thanks for every day....

There is a place that understands, deep within, that violence can only breed more violence and that this is where it must stop. It is not a place where justice means more pain, punishment and revenge. It is rooted in a strong instinct for this depth of pain not to happen to anyone else. The rawness of this wound somehow strips away all that is unimportant. The deepest reality of what it means to be human is laid bare. It is a place of insight which opens up to learning, hope and compassion. It is a place that yearns for healing, which is willing to sacrifice the immediate response of revenge.

It says I know, even right now, in the rawness of this pain and horror, that I am still alive. Alive in a way that I have never been alive before. Alive to possibilities, human possibilities, divine possibilities that there is another way forward that may bring healing to the world. It wants to say, just wait, stay with the pain, let it burn you into a place of renewal. I am always struck and moved by people who have tried to speak out from this place.

In 2003 Marina Cantacuzino asked to interview me for the Forgiveness Project. Here is a quote from the rationale behind the initiative:

In a world where calls for retribution and revenge are the accepted norm, where getting even and acts of spite grab newspaper headlines (whether the stoning to death of an adulteress in Nigeria or mob demonstrations outside a British court), there is a growing and powerful urge to hear stories of reconciliation and forgiveness. These are the really compelling stories of our time, the only ones to capture the public imagination and to inspire.[29]

Marina seemed like a woman after my own heart. I did not hesitate to get involved. Her collection of stories and accompanying photographs (taken by Brian Moody) opened as an exhibition at the Oxo Gallery on the South Bank in London in January 2004. It was called "The F Word". The opening of the exhibition was daunting and exhilarating. It was unnerving to watch people standing in front of the panel with my story and then glance towards me as they recognised the photo. When Archbishop Desmond Tutu (one of the patrons) spoke to me and gave me a huge hug I knew that this was the next step of letting my life speak in the world. Even more affirming was meeting other contributors in the café next door and realising that we had all been treading a rather lonely, treacherous path but now we could rejoice in our meeting and in the birth of a joining-up of purpose.

It was good to meet the sister and mother of Brian McKinney who was abducted by the IRA in 1978. They had also had to wait twenty-one years before finding out the truth of his murder and being able to have a funeral. His mother, Margaret, had kept photos of Brian on top of her wardrobe in the bedroom and cried over them every night, alone. My brother Mark told me that he used to come home sometimes and find Mum doing the same. I remember Mum saying to me once, "I can't go on crying for ever."

Since 2007, I have been working in prisons with the Forgiveness Project. The transformative process continues to change and grow. The collection of stories also continues to grow (read them on the website!). In 2011 they are from the UK, Northern Ireland, South Africa, Palestine and Israel, Canada, USA, New Zealand, Bosnia, Rwanda, Iraq, Hungary, Egypt, Uganda, Senegal, Romania, Pakistan, and the Ukraine.

I work with a team (a minimum of three) as a storyteller and a facilitator. We offer three-day workshops, recently renamed RESTORE (restoration, education, storytelling, team building, openness, respect and empathy). Each workshop invites at least one storyteller to come into prison to share his/her experience of moving towards reconciliation, with course participants. To hear what those who have been harmed by crime have to say is key to establishing empathy and understanding in the group. The honesty, integrity and vulnerability of these stories provide the opportunity for prisoners to be less defended and more open and reflective. They begin to address the harm they have caused and to explore the relationship between themselves as victims, and the victims of their crimes.

On the second day of the workshop I move into my role as a facilitator. The participants have begun a painful process of reflection and are now asked to share aspects of this through mapping out their lives on A3 pieces of paper and presenting their stories to the group. Prisoners are encouraged to "keep safe" and not to reveal issues that they don't want to. However they usually choose to share deep and difficult experiences and traumas. In fact, this is often the first time they have dared to speak personally to a group. It is deeply moving to listen to their stories which are nearly always rooted in a ruined childhood and to witness their feelings as the frozen story begins to thaw. The process is about developing empathy and reducing prejudice. For some prison staff it is also transforming.

Part of the ethos of the Forgiveness Project is that offenders who take part in the programme inside prison have the chance to work for the project when they leave. For the past seven years the project has continued to grow and change. The administration of the charity is overseen by eight trustees. Patrons include Archbishop Desmond Tutu, Emma Thompson,

Terry Waite, Annie Lennox, Tony Benn, and former Lord Chief Justice, Lord Woolf.

Peter Dawson is Governor of HMP High Down. He shared these words in July 2010:

> *For most prisoners, time inside is simply an experience to be endured. So there is something extraordinary about a course which sets out to ask prisoners to examine the most profound and difficult issues imaginable. Attendance brings no privileges or rewards. It often brings heartache. Yet in under three years at HMP High Down, over three hundred prisoners have completed that course, and with no advertisement but word of mouth the number wanting to attend a course has risen from twenty-four in 2007 to eighty-four for the most recent induction day.*
>
> *In my view, the Forgiveness Project can start a process of personal reflection without which rehabilitation and restoration are impossible. It is a privilege for High Down to host such a courageous and compelling undertaking.*

One day I was sitting in my hut, holding Lucy's little woven bag and praying about my work with the Forgiveness Project. I remembered Lucy using thorns to extract thorns from the mess of the raw fleece. Somehow the bag felt alive, as if it had work to do. I began to take it with me into prisons and hand it around as I told our story. It was her gift to me and now it is shared with others as something to hold and contemplate.

The feeling that comes from holding Lucy's little bag is quietly spreading. Softly, "the spirit that delights to do no evil" is truly at work in the realms of *for*-giving. Once I witnessed a man in High Down prison gazing lovingly at the bag, marvelling and not wanting to let go of it and pass it on. He later told me that he didn't usually have experiences like this, but when he had looked at the bag, as it rested between his palms, "there seemed to be light pouring out of it".

The man was Peter Woolf, who spent over eighteen years of his life in prison. It was the first workshop that we facilitated together in High Down prison. We have since worked together in High Down and Parc Prisons. He facilitates many of our workshops. He writes:

The Forgiveness Project is a huge part of my life and has been a crucial part of my long-term rehabilitation and general well-being; to be doing something so worthwhile not only enhances my own self-worth, but it is of massive benefit for others that we (the Forgiveness Project team) continue to show people that there is another way.

My most recent correspondent affected by Lucy's story is also deeply committed to finding a better way forward. He is serving a sentence for stabbing a member of a rival gang. He has also taken to writing poetry. He struggled with his feelings: "I feel bad that it has taken something tragic like this to make me feel positive about myself." I wrote to him and included a supporting letter for his application to Dovegate Prison (the only other therapeutic prison in the country).

I do hope that you are able to go on to HMP Dovegate. It is always moving and encouraging for me to speak in prisons and to realise, again, that no matter what we have been labelled by society ("perpetrators" and "victims") we are ultimately all human beings on a journey towards becoming more human. Labels do not help this process, and the more we cling to them or want to lose them, the further we get from the deeper truth of who we really are when the labels drop away.

I choose to come into prison and share something of my story because I have experienced many times that by sharing our suffering (the truth of our sorrow, our loss) a mysterious process happens. We begin to understand that everyone has this unresolved pain and when we connect with that in others our own pain goes away and healing begins.

Many hands have treasured the little woollen bag, feeling the gentleness, aspiration and hope that it embodies. Many whose hands are stained and clenched by violence, deceit, betrayal, greed, jealousy, hatred and ignorance; many whose hands long to be put to good use, to be valued, who long to be free from shame, have been touched by its simple power. This little woven bag carries something of the generosity and lightness of Lucy's spirit in its wake.

Chapter 11

WORDS OF GRACE

Words couldn't save your life, Lucy, but they are enlarging the place of your aspirations now. Words are close to eternity, travelling across decades, centuries, embodying and evoking fresh meanings, but also resisting the vastness of what is left when words leave. But they have to be found, to crack open that impotent place where not to speak, not to try and find words, seals out life. Words can create, can well up from, an orbit of love.

The response to the words of *Salvaging the Sacred* transformed my life and the life of our family. It has been vital to carrying on. The empowerment of speaking through this essay and trusting the effect of these words "out there" brought a return of the sacred into the heart of our home. Even now I receive letters in response to those words. Some of them need to be in this book. They can't stay still in a drawer. They have work to do. Now it is time to share something of this.

For weeks, large bubble-wrap envelopes with a *The Guardian* sticker in the corner arrived. They didn't fit into the American post box on the road over the bridge on the other side of the river. So the postman had to park the van and walk down the path through the woodland, over the bridge to the front door of our home.

I sat with my children at the kitchen table reading the letters – laughing, crying and amazed. Hundreds and hundreds of letters from all over the country, mostly from people whom we have never met. Some were sharing their grief, some their shame, some were from your university friends whom I had never met. Some sent little presents.

One present was a painted egg with a cockerel, a hen and two chicks, carefully varnished with a little card which simply said, "To replace the egg that was broken, from K.A.W." I had never met this generous, imaginative, person, until the moment of opening the gift. This huge response from friends, extended family and many "strangers" was as affirming as the deep silence at your grave.

One was from Pete, the first boyfriend I had lived with.

I don't know where you are or how to contact you right now. I'll send this to The Mill and hope it gets to you.

I heard the radio. I don't know what you're feeling, I don't know what to say. I don't know who you are living with how many kids you have got. I can't help thinking about you though…

All my memories of you are so unblemished, I am not so proud to think how you must think of me. Hearing about Lucy seemed to plunge me back.

I know I'm one of many people who are wishing to take away a little of the pain. So many people cherished you. I'm sure that hasn't changed.

Who you were, Lucy, before you disappeared, began to enlarge and overlap with a greater memory of you in others. Who you were then is greater than the sum of these memories. This is the story of all who remember you, all who were touched by you. I learnt of someone who fell in love with you:

I met Lucy in the poetry section of a bookshop in Cheltenham in the summer of 1969. Lucy and I started talking about poetry, the poetry we wrote , the things we believed in, and many other things.

Yevtushenko was one of my favourite poets too. I left the shop thinking that Lucy was the most wonderful person I had ever met. I thought she was stunningly attractive and I was excited by the brilliance and insight of her mind. I felt I had never met anyone, at that time, with whom I had such instant, deep and meaningful conversation. I had fallen in love with her.

I loved Lucy's ability to argue with me. I read two of Lucy's poems; one of them was about a churchyard and I can remember the lines which went something like:

> *rolled over saints laid on plates*
> *they weave and wait*

Recently I have hoped that she was buried in the churchyard she described and from your article I suspect that it is so.

Three years ago, Fay, my partner, and our two children were walking near Cheltenham, near where Lucy and I walked. I was thinking about Lucy, not knowing she had ever disappeared. The name Lucy Partington remained very special and precious to me.

Lucy's death, the murder investigations and the trial have been very painful ordeals for me. Part of my difficulty has been that I felt I had no right to such strong emotions of anguish, tenderness, love, loss and anger, because I had known Lucy so briefly. Luckily Fay and a few close friends enabled me to work through these feelings.

...I had worked through a lot of my feelings before I read your article. When I read it I was overwhelmed by the similarity of the picture you drew of Lucy to the one I have carried inside me and described to friends. In that sense your writing had been a source of comfort and joy...

Another old friend of yours had kept a diary at the time when you were together at Exeter. She wrote me a letter, quoting extracts from this diary:

I hope it will not cause you more pain or, in the middle of that pain, at least you may find another little bit extra, of Lucy, that you had not expected, and that was not lost.

22nd February 1972
...Lucy is an unusual-looking person, with curly fly-away hair, a snub nose, blue eyes, and gold-rimmed spectacles. She usually looks severe and intellectual, but when at times the severity relaxes, the lines of her face soften and her eyes grow more vacant, and she's then a little beautiful. She's very intellectual, in a strict, academic sort of way, very literary-minded, analytical and sceptical. Lucy is cynical in a most scornfully positive way about the sort of vocabulary, the way of speaking, that I now accept: "getting it together", "spaced out", "wow", and "really nice" were phrases that came up and were despised by Lucy – which gave me furiously to think...I'd like to speak to Lucy about it more fully.

The letter continued:

What I wrote, I think, shows my respect and my interest in Lucy, my incipient, strong liking for her. I hesitated about sending you this because what I said wasn't always "flattering"- but Lucy would not have been into flattery, and at the time I wrote honestly how she came across to me. I wonder if today I would have used the word "cynical" to describe Lucy? (I'm trying hard to look back into remembering essence-of-Lucy.) It's hard to say. The phrase that springs to mind in the language I would use today (sadly fallen from the lofty heights of university-speak) is that Lucy was a brilliant bullshit-buster. She could spot a bullshitter a mile off. I think it was her qualities of clarity and honesty, her refusal to compromise for the sake of clubbability, that attracted me to her and makes her stand out in my memory as a unique and special person...at the time I sensed in her a kindred spirit.

Having thought so much about Lucy the last couple of years, and gone over and over my memories of her, I was so delighted to recognise her in your writing. I was enchanted that Lucy thought of you as an incorrigible romantic. It is extraordinary to me that, although I had limited contact with Lucy, the few images I have of her, both her face and her personality, are so vivid, strong and alive. She bounces through my memory with great vigour and robustness, three-dimensional. I know that I did not forget her, and never will.

Later on when Mrs. Humphreys at Staylittle Stores asked to read the Guardian essay, you travelled around the local Welsh farming community. When the magazine was eventually returned your face was tattooed with a sum of pencilled numbers. I could just imagine a farmer grabbing the nearest piece of paper to jot down a business calculation. It reminded me of our childhood and our times at Gretton Farm and put it all into an everyday proportion.

Your friend Penny wrote to me about Yevtushenko.

I was deeply affected by your mention of Yevtushenko. I have loved his work for the last twenty-five years or so without acknowledging where I first came across him. Lucy and I visited you in Bristol and, if my memory is to be trusted, in your room you had a painting with a Yevtushenko poem written across it. Then I remember I bought myself the very same edition of poems that you had bought Lucy and of course still have it.

Your friend Lizzie Christie had told me about your favourite poem in the book, *I Hung a Poem on a Branch*. I had written in *Salvaging the Sacred* about my dream vision inspired by this poem. It was at the time of Rosemary West's trial when I knew the air would be thick with spotted words. At the end of the essay I invited people to take action:

Maybe we could start with each one of us writing a favourite poem on a small piece of cloth and tying it to a tree in memory of all victims of violence, and as an act towards hope for a world in which cruelty is replaced by compassion.

Many people responded to the idea of hanging a poem on a tree in uniquely creative ways. Thousands and thousands of words flapped in the wind, like seeds, fanning the sacred. Nothing negative ever came out of the sharing of those words. Only an orbit of light and love, wrapping us in warmth. It felt as if the place of the words that arose within me had been responded to from the same place in others. An honouring of the good, the "kynde", of all that is our true home; purifying the pollution of our national consciousness, in the wake of the media coverage. Our humanity was raised by this spontaneous offering of all that is beneficial. They had to be returned, hung out there on trees bearing witness to the core of our humanity. They proclaim a body of truth carrying that which is essential for renewal. They speak of grace, of our potential world.

The cloak of poems wrapped us with the compassion of friends and strangers. I wept with gratitude and wonder at the mystery and miracle of it all. A gleaming, beckoning me on towards a gleaning.

I re-read the poem again.

> *I hung a poem*
> > *on a branch.*
> *Thrashing,*
> > *it resists the wind.*
> *"Take it down,*
> > *don't joke,"*
> > > *you urge.*
> *People pass.*
> > *Stare in surprise.*
> *Here's a tree*
> > *waving*
> > > *a poem.*
> *Don't argue now.*
> > *We have to go on.*
> *"You don't know it by heart!"...*
> > > *"That's true,*
> *but I'll write a fresh poem for you tomorrow."*
> *It's not worth being upset by such trifles!*
> *A poem's not too heavy for a branch.*
> *I'll write as many as you ask for,*
> *As many poems*
> > *as there are trees!*
> *How shall we get on in the future together?*
> *Perhaps we shall soon forget this?*
> *No,*
> > *if we have trouble on the way,*
> *we'll remember*
> > *that somewhere,*

> bathed in light
>
> a tree
>
> is waving
>
> a poem,
>
> and smiling we'll say:
>
> "We have to go on ..."
>
> **Yevgeny Yevtushenko**

Somehow this poem reminds me of the power of creativity to probe the stagnant clods of fear into a welling up of a trusting vision that soothes and inspires. It provides me with an image that suggests the infinite resources within me to find and offer hope and beauty in the face of the horror of your death. It's something about having to leave behind what we didn't quite catch or commit to heart during a moment that isn't quite resolved or understood. Trust it to the wind, trust the public gesture, knowing that we have to go on, but that our inner resources will bring more poems, as many poems as there are trees.

I don't know if Yevtushenko ever came across Tibetan prayer flags. Tibetan culture is wrapped in the cloth of prayer. Their Buddhist symbols and mantras brighten rocks, fill deities, saturate the air. In Buddhist practice all thought, speech and action are informed by the attention of prayer. The gradual cultivation of this attitude towards whatever arises in my life has informed my way forward. A murmur of love and prayer was calling out from the most brutal of stories, dissolving that which is sticky and staining.

The day that *Salvaging the Sacred* was published I was sitting under a tree at the May festival in Newtown. My friend Maria handed me a dog-eared envelope. She had already read the essay and shown it to a visiting poet who had done his performance and was rushing off to catch a train. He had scrawled this extract from one of his poems in biro. It was Adrian Mitchell, whom I had heard at the Edinburgh Festival in 1969. They were the first words to return. From someone with a deep love and commitment to words, like us.

especially when it snows
and down the purple pathways of the sky
the planet staggers like King Lear
with his dead darling in his arms

especially when it snows
and keeps on snowing
Adrian Mitchell

In May 2004, I went on my third and final retreat with Master Sheng Yen. This time it was in Switzerland. For three days it snowed and snowed and kept on snowing. An image of him remains in my mind. He stood with us outside in freezing conditions, his gentle Chinese voice flowing into the cold air, the silent pauses, between his words in Chinese and the interpreter's translation, like the spaces between the falling snow. His shaved head was bare with no hat, yet he was perfectly at ease. The rest of us were shivering, bundled up, restless and cold, longing to return to the Chan Hall.

On this retreat there was an experience of the subtle persistence of my demanding ego. The pain in my legs became so intense that I began to be convinced that if I didn't stand up, immediately, my knees would be permanently damaged. But I applied the practice and investigated the pain. By moving towards it, connecting with it, making friends with it, I felt it changing, dissolving, leaving me free to continue sitting. The snow continued, the bell rang, the session ended.

After the retreat I stayed on for a week in a nearby Swiss valley where spring was bursting out with the creamy-brown cows who were being herded back into the bright, lush meadows. I walked up to higher pastures and wrote a letter.

The shadow of the pen moved across the paper carrying a faint scratching: each mark clear and precise. As I approached the paper with less effort, words rose and fell. Looking up into the sky, I traced the ascent of the forest on the mountain beyond, the fresh green faded into bare rock. A few dark pines softened the edges of the rocks beneath the summit where the eternal snow gleamed in shining silence. Above this yearning forest the peaks of white clouds slowly created a ravine, a lake, of blue sky, shifting with a time that drifts like continents.

Whatever arises is how it is. Bird song seems fuller, clearer. The plastic water bottle creaks, expanding in the noon heat. The air carries a coolness from the snow above. Flower blooms bristle with fragile life in a gust of wind. A smile changes the shape of my face. A bubble of laughter travels up from somewhere deep inside. There is a respect that allows no hatred, coming from a deep ease.

Friday May 7th 2004
Beatenberg Waldegg, Interlaken, Switzerland
Dear Rosemary,
It has taken me ten years to write this letter. When my sister Lucy disappeared from the bus stop near Pitville Park in Cheltenham she was twenty-one years old and you were nineteen years old. That was now thirty-one years ago. I don't know the whole truth about Lucy's murder. You have denied being involved in it.

I have not met you, and know very little about you, apart from the crimes which you deny committing, the abuse that you suffered as a child from your brother and father, and the abduction and rape you suffered when you were fifteen years old. It is difficult to get a real picture of you as a whole person. I do hope that you continue to be helped and supported in some way.

After laying Lucy to rest with the love and honour that she deserved, I have been trying to face the reality of the way in which she died. I accept that I will probably never know the missing details of her journey from the bus stop to her final dismemberment and burial in the basement of 25 Cromwell Street, Gloucester. I have been seeking to know how to be free of any feelings of anger and bitterness towards you.

At last I can write to tell you something that you may not understand but which may help you too in some way. I can honestly say that at times I feel a strange sort of gratitude towards you, because a true compassion for the terrible suffering that you have created by your actions, for yourself and so many other people.

I have been making this journey with the help of Buddhist retreats from the Chan tradition, and many other people. It helps me to face myself and move towards a truth which helps me to transform the effect of my mistakes into a way of living that brings some healing.

When I vowed to try to forgive you on my first Chan retreat with Master Sheng Yen in 1995 I experienced murderous rage shortly afterwards. Somehow I knew that I could have killed someone too. My inner work began in earnest. I realised that I needed to train myself to lessen the harm that I can do to my own life and the lives of others by facing my own greed, hatred and ignorance.

Now, I am sitting in the mountains in Switzerland, at the end of my eleventh retreat. We sit in silence for seven days observing and investigating what arises within ourselves, accepting it, facing it, dealing with it and letting it go. Gradually our bodies and minds begin to relax. The Buddhist teachings point us towards the reality that everything is changing in every moment and that nothing is inherently separate from anything else. Gradually my self-centred attitude towards life lessens and my heart opens into a more spacious, natural way of being alive. I feel grateful to be alive. It feels like unpeeling layers of an onion.

I don't know what the centre is, but when I went for a walk in the forest I saw a branch bowed down by the weight of fresh snow. As I walked by, my shoulder brushed against it and the snow fell softly to the ground. The branch sprang up, free from its burden. Maybe that is what the centre is? A release into how we are naturally meant to be – at ease. I have a long way to go and I would not be making this journey if my dear sister had not suffered a terrible death, maybe at your hands.

I have made choices in my life that have hurt other people, especially when I was feeling deep confusion and pain about Lucy's inexplicable disappearance. Life seemed so strange. How could someone just disappear, for twenty years?

I know that you have known a lot of fear. You said that you felt that you had been always looking over your shoulder, all your life. I feel fear in my belly. Sometimes I feel heavy and black. When I looked at the mountains yesterday, I saw my heart. Some of it is still frozen like the snow on the peaks, some of it has melted into the lake at the bottom of the valley. Sometimes it catches the sun and shines.

I am sending you these words in the hope that they may help you in some way. Please know that I do not feel any hostility towards you, just a sadness, a deep sadness that all this has happened, and that your heart could not feel a truth that I wish you could know.

Our lives are connected and I am sending you the springing of the branch as a token of hope. May you be less burdened by fear.

I continued to walk, alone, up into the mountains where the snow was melting and spring flowers were beginning to open in the alpine meadows. There was a freshness of newly-growing grasses and flowers. Some flowers I could not name. It was enough to be filled with a knowledge of swaying blades, stalks and blossoms, gentle and brilliant, merging as if in silent communication. The soft sound of cow-bells floated up from the valley far below. Bird song rose and fell. A woodpecker drilled a tree trunk nearby.

In 2008, four years later, I posted the letter to Rosemary West. It seemed like the right time to do it. I had waited until I did not expect or need to have a reply. On my return from the annual Quaker camp two letters awaited me. One was in an envelope addressed in my handwriting. I had enclosed this envelope in a letter to Mum at Rosebank Care Home near Oxford, near my birthplace. In 2007 Mum had been diagnosed with dementia and later Parkinsons Disease and had eventually gone into residential care. By this time she hardly spoke and was becoming very thin. Her hand trembled and rotated with the typical Parkinson's tremor. In my letter to her I had encouraged her to write something to me, but had not expected a reply.

The other envelope looked official and contained these words:

Kalyx[33]
HMP
30/07/08
Dear Marian Partington,
Subject: letter dated 24/07/08 to Ms Rose West
Ms West has received your letter and asked me to relay a message on her behalf and asked that you please cease all correspondence, she does not wish to receive any further letters from you.
Any further letters sent will be kept in Security.
Yours Sincerely…

Inside the other envelope were five shaky words, Mum's final written words:

I love you, from Mum XXX

The garden at The Mill came to mind. It was shining with the ordered maturity of fifty years of her devoted tending. Blackbirds and wood pigeons were singing up Spring. The lawn curved around the pond, edging the banks of daffodils, narcissi and hellebores, in yellows, whites and shades of green. Celandines were defying the wood chippings here and there amidst a blaze of pink rockroses, forget-me-nots (the blue that is unforgettable), a white flowering shrub (by now I should know these names), planted and given in memory of David (our stepfather) who died in 2002 on St David's Day. He had managed to drive around the beloved grounds on his tractor, capturing the early Spring buds on his digital camera a few days before he died in his chair by the fire, after a glass of whisky and *The Archers*, waiting for Mum to bring his supper: leeks from the garden in cheese sauce, which he never ate. Mum had gardened on, as she always has. "Thrashing about in the garden" she called it. As she used to say, "The grass keeps growing." As the sun sinks she puts me to weed near the vegetable patch, separating the roots of the celandines and throwing them into the wheelbarrow, easing the earth around the maroon shoots of peonies. The newly-cut lawn shines with a fresh green beneath the pear blossoms' creamy tresses, perfectly open, hinting at the golden pears to come. A silent robin approaches.

Epilogue

*Acknowledging the experience you share is the only thing that opens up the possibility of finding a meaning that can be shared, a language to speak together.*34
Rowan Williams

The richness of my experience has been humbling and mysterious, perhaps best conveyed in the language of dreams. This is the speech of Jung's "collective unconscious". The Greeks saw dreams as a meeting place for the living and the dead. As Jung's friend Laurens van der Post suggests:

*It is as if the individual memory is enclosed in a greater which even in the night of our forgetfulness stands like an angel with folded wings at the ready, at the moment of acknowledged need, to guide us back to the lost spoor of our meanings.*35

The imagery of all the dreams spoke of varying degrees of *dis-* and *re-*. The words of the water meadow dream seemed to come from a well of healing deep in the heart of consciousness that is a natural aspect of creative imagination. This realm is timeless, effortless, harmonising and spontaneous. It is a way of knowing that exists beyond comprehension. It is a way of remembering who we really are. It is a place of communion with the myriad flux of all forms of life; forms that arise and dissolve, come and go. It speaks of grace. Is it "our dream"?

The opportunity to be changed during the Crisis was informed by the skeleton dream which led to the action of the wrapping of Lucy's bones. This was the solemn language of silent reclamation and celebration, the embracing of the dead remains of my sister, hidden for so long. This was the complex physical frame that carries the unique form of our flesh: the muscles, the tendons, the ligaments, the organs, the blood – all that quickly rots away. This was the waking up to the physical reality of impermanence and transformation. This physical body will die and it will be reduced to bones, dust and ashes. It could happen at any time. So who am I?

Confessing involved accepting the excruciating paradox that by attempting to grapple with and enfold the effect upon me of the atrocity of Lucy's fate, by struggling to bring her true name to light, my own destructiveness, woundings and delusions were laid bare, unfolded and revealed. The light reveals the darkest nooks and crannies. The "doll baby" in the dream needed to speak, eat, trust, live, and flourish. What lay beneath in the plaster mask dream? I could not avoid self-confrontation. My defended reality was eroded relentlessly, painfully and hopelessly. There was no turning away again. What is in the way of knowing who I am?

Comprehending that the "hope of a better past" is a convenient delusion, an ignorant deceit, was intertwined with a need to confess shame and guilt. But there was also the need to profess a trust and faith in the greater whole of the creative imagination that connects and quickens us all. The reality that we are one interdependent, fragile body brings an acute, vital need to behave with wisdom and compassion. This is radical transformation. The sea dream told me: "I keep throwing them into the sea but the waves keep bringing them back." Maybe the biggest "sin" is the biggest delusion: to believe and behave as if we are at the centre of the universe, with separate fixed identities. The *dis-* (apart, asunder, isolated, shrunken) within me moved towards the *re-* (afresh, anew, connected, alive).

Transforming moments involved a movement from the small self into "the larger self of the whole universe". The moment of authentic empathy for Rosemary West was simultaneously reciprocated by a feeling of having been released. While I was experiencing this compassion (empathy with suffering), my isolated pain was transformed into a feeling of spacious ease that connected me with all forms of life. In that moment *forgiving* came to life. This inner transformation led to the outer work in prisons. It was rooted in the water meadow dream, as if the lotus flower, anchored in the mud, had eventually opened, had pushed itself out of the mud and the water into the air and the sky. *Pearl* is the jewel in the heart of the lotus, the pearl of great price.

Once I "saw" Lucy as an angel (not quite seeing, as if out of the corner of my eye, a different kind of seeing). She was in a meadow in Switzerland, after the last retreat with Master Sheng Yen. I had just written the letter to Rosemary West. It was above a grassy mound near some beehives. There was a sound of bees, a soft breeze, spring sunshine. She was hot-sun-sky-blue, Virgin Mary blue, elongated and as large as the medieval image of St Christopher in Hailes church. Her wings were slightly lifted, she was smiling, gleaming and hovering but still (in the way of hawks). She said, "Thank you for everything that you have been doing for me, Marian. Now all you have to do is to watch the seeds grow." And she left. This moment felt like the transformation of our relationship as sisters into the "larger self of the whole universe". Within me, Lucy has become the "Light" of her name. The ultimate reality of my Dharma name, given to me by Chan Master Sheng Yen in 1995, *Guo Guang*, means the result of light 果光居士. We are not separate. Something continues beyond the physical form.

I had managed to remain unmarried for most of my life. This had been a conscious choice. I had witnessed the bitter disintegration of my parents' marriage when I was twelve, I was averse to a meaningless secular commitment, and I was strongly influenced by the feminist culture. But gradually I realised that it was also a selfish, outworn, obstinate choice.

In 2007, Nick and I had a Buddhist blessing during a retreat on Holy Island, followed by a Quaker wedding.

The blessing took place on the fourth day of the retreat. We sat on our colourful Holy Island cushions, floating on our bright Tibetan mats, accompanied by the sound of the sea and the seabirds, side by side in front of John Crook and the altar with the *Sangha* (the Buddhist word for community) seated on three sides. The blessing began with a confession, "to clean the slate". This was helpful and felt clarifying.

All the harm committed by me stemming from body, speech and mind I hereby openly confess. I acknowledge errors of greed, desire and ignorance and seek the selfless expression of our true natures for the benefit of each other and for us all.

Then my response to John's question "Why get married now?"

Making a vow of marriage at this stage in our long relationship of 26 years as lovers, partners, friends and parents feels like a ripening of something that has continued through thick and thin, which requires honouring and celebrating. It cannot be contained by words.

It is a gesture of gratitude to Nick and all those who have shared our lives, and a gesture of trust and hope that this ripening may continue until we drop off the branch.

Rilke describes the relationship of marriage as offering to be guardians of each other's solitude. We both feel at home with these words.

We are making this commitment for the benefit of all sentient beings, as a gesture towards peace and health, within the walls of this hall (the Centre for Peace and Health) on this Holy Island, thus contributing to the regeneration of that which is sacred. Thank you for your presence in this blessed moment.

We all chanted *Om Mane Padme Hum* 108 times and then John sprinkled us (he called it "asperging") with two gull's feathers from the beach dipped in water purified with saffron. Raising our faces to receive the droplets of water felt humbling, unifying and timeless. Happiness and rejoicing arose. There were tears and hugs and great warmth. The sun was shining outside as we held hands. We all returned to our cushions with warm hearts. It was good to continue the retreat and not get caught up in too much self-indulgence. It felt perfect. Later that night, the new moon and the planet Venus hung like the Muslim symbol in the sky with the sound of sea birds settling.

The ripples of that blessing continue in our hearts. We received a beautiful card with a photo of us both, kneeling together, laughing, side by side, with John grinning above us with the feathers and the bowl of water and his priestly stole forming a collar on his robe. By the picture are the words:

> *The things that matter in our lives are not fantastic or grand. They are the moments when we touch one another...*

Our Quaker wedding a few months later was an opportunity to bring together many friends and family to bear witness to our Quaker vows to be "loving and faithful....through divine assistance... so long as we both on earth shall live." The vows were spoken within the silence of a Quaker meeting for worship. The celebrations at home in the evening afterwards were full of music, feasting, dancing and entertainments offered by guests. The celebrations continued for two more days. We were blessed by a heat wave after weeks of torrential rain. Everyone I looked at on the day of the wedding was smiling. It was as if this is how we are really meant to be, loving and well-wishing, celebratory, fully alive.

Two and a half years later, Mum died peacefully. A week before she died, she gave her last gift to me and my dear brothers, in turn. It was a transfiguring smile that gathered us in love.

As Marian, I am of Mary. I felt drawn to and sat with many carved, painted, wooden images of her with Christ on her knee, both gazing directly towards me, in the Medieval Romanesque churches on my pilgrimage to Santiago de Compostela during the Autumn of 2010. They radiated a transcendent mixture of peace, joy and a stillness that was arresting, beckoning and refreshing, that encouraged me to give thanks for my life and to simply keep walking towards the "field of stars" and the tomb of St. James, one of Christ's apostles, maybe his cousin. The Romanesque churches were perfect spaces for the echoing back and swirling around of notes from my shakuhachi flute. The flute's notes were my prayer.

The community of pilgrims was truly global, humorous and ever-changing. There was not much to hang on to as the miles slipped behind me and the names of the places and images receded into insignificance. The further I walked the more "ordinary" I became. Leaving before dawn and walking with the stars, being guided by the brightest, Jupiter, in the West, watching it fade with the rising sun that warmed my back, and suffused the landscape with capillaries of fresh, red light. There was a feeling of belonging and a feeling of passing through. Just the walking, the breathing, the feeling of joy and freedom and the feeling that everything that has ever been is who I am now, with every step and every breath. Reciting Tibetan mantras, singing the chorus of the medieval pilgrim song, *Ultreia*.

Walking, walking, passing through towns, villages, cities, over rivers and mountains, through woods, vineyards, *la meseta* desert (where brown insects hopped high into the air opening their dazzling turquoise wings). Walking, walking, passing through orchards of peaches, apples, walnuts, apricots, chestnuts. Walking, walking, passing through heat, rain, mist, moonlight. Walking, walking, with lives of those in the past who walked this way, lives of those in the present from all over the world, lives of those in the future. Walking, walking, watch out for bedbugs and blisters; the fears of heat, getting lost, not arriving, getting ill – all these dropped away. Walking, walking with the changing leaves and the harvest, for six hundred miles, for thirty-eight days. This journey could simply not be made without all that was arising in every step, all who travel this way with human frailty learning more about humility, faith, hope, and love.

The giant censer that swung from ceiling to ceiling like a huge pendulum across the transept of the cathedral in Santiago was in great contrast to the solemn Catholic mass. It was like a trapeze act that billowed its clouds of incense with gusto and daring, offering vigorous purification of *dis*-ease and a timeless completion. It was humbling, amusing, triumphant and awe-inspiring.

Wind gathers in the cloth, a flapping of flames. Clasp the mast, a bliss of birds bulging the cloth. The hands that worked to the bone: harvesting, spinning, weaving the flax; sewing colours into the cloth, emblems of saints; blessing the sails. Leave these hands on the shore. Earth shifts in the roots, a land falling away. Trust the sail, its bright signs unfolding, cloaking the wind. *Re*-member the water meadow, the field of stars where

if you sit very still, you can hear the sun move.

Whether I like it or not, (but I do love it and sing praise for it) "our" water meadow dream has planted its weight with increasing bulk like a smooth boulder from the River Trannon (fast-flowing) by our house. When the river is low I can sit very still on this old rock and contemplate the sound of the water gushing, eroding a few grains of gravel a year. In full blood, the flood hurls pebbles, chipping, faceting. The water dyes flesh deep-orange, like Seville marmalade. It comes down from the peat moors above our valley. It feeds into the Severn. Centuries from now, the boulder will rest as gravel on the riverbed. It will hardly respond to the current, settling into a vein of silt. What really matters?

Things are as big as you make them -
I can fill a whole body,
a whole day of life
with worry
about a few words
on one scrap of paper;
yet, the same evening,
looking up,
can frame my fingers
to fit the sky
in my cupped hands.

Lucy Partington 1952–1973

Notes

PROLOGUE

1 Lucy's edition was E. V. Gordon, ed., *Pearl* (London: Oxford University Press, 1953), now superseded by Malcolm Andrew and Ronald Waldron, eds., *The Poems of the* Pearl *Manuscript: Pearl, Cleanness, Patience, Sir Gawain and the Green Knight* (Exeter: University of Exeter Press, rev. 5th ed., 2007) with a prose translation on CD-ROM. ISBN 978-0859897914

2 Paul Piehler, *Pearl*, in *The Visionary Landscape: A Study in Medieval Allegory* (London: Edward Arnold, 1971) 19. ISBN 0713155795

3 Marian Partington, *Salvaging the Sacred: Lucy, My Sister* (London: Quaker Books, 2004) ISBN 0852453531. Originally published in *The Guardian Weekend* 18th May 1996, and reprinted in *The Guardian Year '96*, ed. Georgina Henry (London: Fourth Estate, 1996) 140–160

4 Professor Avril Henry: *An Appreciation of Lucy Partington* at Lucy's requiem mass, Exeter University 16th February 1995

5 His Holiness the Dalai Lama, *Kindness, Clarity and Insight* trans. Jeffrey Hopkins (Ithaca, NY, USA: Snow Lion Publications, 1984) 103. This is one of eight verses from the 11th Century Tibetan text by gLang-ri-thang-pa: *Eight Stanzas for Training the Mind*

6 Matthew 5:44, The Bible. Authorised King James Version

CHAPTER 4

7 Yevgeny Aleksandrovich Yevtushenko, *Early Poems by Yevgeny Yevtushenko*, ed. and trans. George Reavey (London: Marion Boyars, 1969, 2009) ISBN 978-0714528960

8 www.catherineblountfdn.org

CHAPTER 5

9 David Self, *Struggling with Forgiveness: Stories from People and Communities* (Toronto: Path Books, 2003) 156. ISBN 1551263955

10 J. D. Schumacher, *Helping Children Cope with a Sibling's Death*, in *Death and Grief in the Family*, ed. James C. Hansen and Thomas T. Frantz, The Family Therapy Collections, 8 (Rockville, Md.: Aspen Systems Corporation, 1984)

11 N. Abraham and M. Torok, *The Shell and the Kernel*, trans. Nicholas T. Rand (Chicago: University of Chicago Press, 1994) 171. ISBN 0226000885

12 David Self, *Struggling with Forgiveness*, page 21

13 James Gilligan, *Violence: reflections on a national epidemic* (New York: Vintage Books, 1997) 64–66

14 David Self, *Struggling with Forgiveness*, page 156

CHAPTER 6

15 Primo Levi, *The Drowned and the Saved* (London: Sphere Books Ltd., 1989) 64-65. ISBN 0349100470

16 Genesis 2, The Bible. Authorised King James Version

17 Gary Snyder, *Good, Wild, Sacred* (Hereford: Five Seasons Press, 1984) 26. ISBN 0947960007

18 Samuel Hahnemann, *The Organon of Medicine*, trans. R. E. Dudgeon (New Delhi: B. Jain Publishers Ltd., reprint 1986) 33

CHAPTER 7

19 Gabi Mihalache, *Transformative Forgiveness: A Heuristic Study of the Self-transforming Nature of Becoming Forgiving Following Traumatic Events* (US: ProQuest Information & Learning Publishing, 2008) 167. ISBN 978-0549841319

20 In 1997 The Western Chan Fellowship (www.westernchan fellowship.org) was formed as an association of western lay Chan practitioners running retreats, meditation groups and a publication (New Chan Forum). Dr. John Crook received Dharma transmission from Chan Master Sheng Yen in 1993, Dr. Simon Child received transmission in 2000. On July 15th 2011 John died. It was the day that this book went off to readers. It was hoped that he would write an introduction, as my teacher and patient supporter of this "writing project", as he referred to it. He now has the posthumous accolade of Chan Master, to my knowledge the first westerner to receive this title. Dr. Simon Child is now the Teacher of the WCF.

21 A bodhisattva aspires and works towards enlightenment so that others may be free from suffering:
For as long as space endures, And for as long as living beings remain, Until then may I too abide, To dispel the misery of the world.
From *A Guide to the Bodhisattva's Way of Life*, Shantideva, trans. Stephen Batchelor (Ithaca: Snow Lion, rev. 6th ed., 1992) ISBN 978-8185102597

CHAPTER 8

22 Hung-Chih Cheng Chueh, *On Silent Illumination,* quoted in Master Sheng-Yen, *The Method of No-Method* trans. Guogu (Boston: Shambala, 2006) 20. ISBN 978-1590305751
23 A hexagram is a stack of six lines, consisting of two trigrams (three lines). There are 64 different combinations of *yin* (divided line) and *yang* (undivided line). Each hexagram is a picture or image of moral, social, psychological and philosophical themes. They are formed by clustering and dividing yarrow stalks or throwing three coins. For more information see Adeline Yen Mah, *Watching the Tree* (London: Harper Collins Publishers, reprint 2011) ISBN 978-0006531548
24 Trans. Richard Wilhelm, *The I Ching* (London: Routledge & Kegan Paul Ltd., 1968) 203
25 Sanskrit word meaning "action", understood as the law of causality. According to the Buddha's teaching, all actions, whether of thought, word or deed, are like seeds which will eventually bear fruit in terms of experience, in this or future lives. A positive, virtuous action will result in happiness, while the definition of sin or negative action is that which causes suffering later on.

CHAPTER 9

26 George Herbert, *Love,* in *The English Poems of George Herbert*, ed. Helen Wilcox (Cambridge: Cambridge University Press, 2007) 661. ISBN 978-0521868211

CHAPTER 10

27 All names are changed for the sake of privacy.
28 His pioneering project, "Restorative Justice in Prisons", involved three prisons: Bristol, Norwich and Winchester. I was invited to work with a team in Bristol (Horfield) prison. My role was to raise victim awareness amongst staff and prisoners.
29 www.theforgivenessproject.com
30 Peter Woolf, *The Damage Done* (London: Bantam, 2009) ISBN 978-0553819335

CHAPTER 11

31 See Chapter 4, Re-earthing, page 54
32 Adrian Mitchell, *Blue Coffee* (Newcastle upon Tyne: Bloodaxe Books, 1996) 160. ISBN 1852243627
33 Kalyx is an organization that provides custody and care for male and female prisoners. It is a private prison.

EPILOGUE

34 Rowan Williams, *Writing in the Dust* (London: Hodder and Stoughton, 2002) 73. ISBN 978-0340787199
35 Laurens van der Post, *The Lost World of the Kalahari* (London: Vintage Classics, 2011) ISBN 978-0099428756
36 Jack Kornfield, *A Path with Heart* (London: Ebury Publishing, 2002) 14. ISBN 978-0712657808
37 A traditional Japanese bamboo flute played in medieval times by the Fuke sect of Zen Buddhism. The *komuso* (priests of nothingness) played the shakuhachi as a method of spiritual practice. The purer the breath becomes, the more the monk is "empty of self".
38 This is a medieval expression of encouragement and joy, a way of greeting fellow pilgrims: *Ultreia, ultreia, sus eia, Deus adjuvanos*: Going on beyond, going on beyond, and upwards, God is approaching us.
It reminds me of the Sanskrit mantra from the Buddhist Heart Sutra:
Gate gate, paragate, parasamgate, bodhi svaha: Go, go, go beyond, go thoroughly beyond and establish yourself in enlightenment.

Acknowledgements

This book has been evolving for eighteen years. It would not be here without the good will, aspirations and efforts of others. There are almost innumerable people, communities and landscapes to be acknowledged. Many I will never meet or know.

I begin with gratitude for the spiritual lineages of east and west that have offered guidance, strength, wisdom and discipline. I name and thank the teachers from whom I have had the great fortune to learn, and also acknowledge all who have travelled with me.

I bow to Chan Masters Sheng Yen and Dr. John Crook and the Western Chan Fellowship. Śrāmaṇeri Jinhoshi, a Taiwanese Chan Buddhist nun, who came regularly to our home to run retreats. Professor Terayama Tanchu, Zen calligraphy master, and his disciple Sarah Moate with special thanks for the teaching of the Zen line (mujibo) and 無東西 (Mu-tō-zai, or No-East-West). Mike McInerney, my shakuhachi teacher. Barbara Richter, teacher and practitioner of Qi Gong, Tai Chi and acupuncture, and a steadfast, imaginative, invaluable friend for nearly forty years. I am deeply indebted to Sister

Ruth Furneaux, an Anglican contemplative nun, who initiated the Morning Star Sangha, a group of people involved in the exploration of Buddhist/Christian interpractice. Archbishop Rowan Williams, whose humility, writing, friendship and shining faith brought me to another level of attention. Brother Nicholas, and all the Brothers of the Society of St Francis, at Glasshampton Monastery, whose humble hospitality and joyful, contemplative lives have provided an anchor and refuge for the past eight years. The retreat time spent there with a wonderful group of women friends has been deeply nourishing. Monsignor George Hay, Lucy's Catholic priest, for his prayerful support and refreshing humour. The many Quakers whose unprejudiced, faithful example upheld the imperative to "let your life speak" and trust that there is "that of God" in everyone.

I will always be deeply grateful for the generous financial and spiritual support that enabled this journey of contemplation and writing to continue. A deep thank you to the Joseph Rowntree Charitable Trust, especially the trustee Marion McNaughton, whose willingness to invest in the invisible process of healing to allow the right words led to unexpected, fruitful places. My support group at this time (Alison Leonard, Iris Tute and Jan Caine) who upheld me and listened with great tenderness. The Allen Lane Foundation, for their generous grant. I especially thank one trustee, Jane Walsh, with whom I listened to Richard Holloway's talk on his book on forgiveness, at the Hay Festival.

Now I turn to all those who have engaged and grappled with this complex subject with such open, questing hearts. With respect and gratitude to all those at the International Conference on Forgiveness at Findhorn in October 1999 who affirmed the global importance of this subject and the value of my voice within that discourse. To the participants of the first International Conference on Restorative Justice in Winchester in March 2001, where my inner journey found an outer form. Special thanks to Tim Newell who invited me to contribute to his innovative project Restorative Justice in Prisons. To "the team" in Bristol prison (Marian Liebmann, Barbara Tudor and Lindy Wootton) and all the prisoners who dared to change. To the philosopher, Dr Michael Bavidge, with whom I took up a probing correspondence after a conference on *Perspectives on Evil and Human Wickedness*. To Professor Phil Scraton who asked me to contribute to five ESRC funded research seminars (*Disasters: Origins, Consequences and Responses*). It was moving and healing to meet and share with others who have suffered traumatic loss, from Dunblane and Hillsborough.

Then the wordsmiths (journalists, editors, writers) without whom there would be no book. Deborah Orr, journalist and editor of the Guardian Weekend in 1996, who delivered the first essay, *Salvaging the Sacred*, into the public domain with sensitivity and integrity. The generous response to this essay changed my life in a radical way and encouraged me to continue. Melissa Benn for her three part radio series, *Forgive and Forget?* (May 2001). She seemed to choose just the right words from our long interview and put them in just the right place. Canon David Self, whose interview for his book, *Struggling with Forgiveness*, gave me a new perspective and helped me to feel understood and accepted within a Christian context. Christine Clegg, who invited me into the academic discourse with my piece *Letter to Lucy: you know that dream we had last night* for the journal *new formations*. An ever thankful smile to Canon Stephen Cherry whose invitation to contribute to his book *Healing Agony* and response to my writing has been affirming and stimulating. Marina Cantacuzino is owed huge thanks for her tenacious, undaunting commitment to the Forgiveness Project and for her gentle heart, which remains open to the pain and complexity of this subject. She has collected and given voice to many storytellers who have dared to open themselves to this adventurous, demanding work.

I am indebted to the anonymous writer of *Pearl* and all who have engaged with these dazzling words as scholars, translators and lovers of medieval English literature. Also to Robert Wynne-Simmons whose passionate love of *Pearl* has taken him on many scholarly and creative adventures. He invited me to share, as he described it, "a little oasis at the British Library, when everything cleared a space for a look at the *Pearl* facsimile". This moment inspired the present shape of the book. But it was Emeritus Professor Avril Henry, Lucy's tutor at Exeter University in 1973, who bravely took up the beginning of the task to shape my writing into the form of this book. Her courageous offer to read my work, and her enthusiasm for my idea for the structure, brought the book back to life. We worked together intensely for a while. It was an important discipline and a poignant exploration for which I remain utterly grateful.

However it was when Sarah Bird, whom I had first encountered on a Buddhist retreat, asked if she could read my book, that it found its perfect editor and publisher. Sarah's professional editorial skills and Vala's fresh, innovative vision of community supported publishing were just what the book had been waiting for. Her passionate commitment and her editorial standards have been sensitive, unflinching, courageous, patient and intuitive. The motto "less is more" has been liberating, reminding me of the heart of the creative process. I also thank the following members of the Vala co-op, whose minute attention refined the final manuscript: Fi Radford, Phil Seal, Pat Simmons, Kerry Vernon, and Denis Kennedy. Finally, I thank the careful, imaginative artist Sue Gent, whose skill has brought the book into full being.

Heartfelt thanks to the many true friends whose loving support helps me to trust what arises. To name a few: Chloë Keef, Rosie de Bree, Jacqueline Tong, Sally Mitchison and John Charlton, Ron Simpson, Paul Taylor, Catherine Henderson, David and Jenny Jones, Julie Hodgson, Sasha Kagan, Jo Lumley, David and Marianne John and Allan Holmes. To Lucy's childhood friends who have become my friends: Lizzie Christie, Angela Drinkwater Lunn, Helly Bliss and Beryl Smith. To Guy Chapman who generously gave us the hut, in which much of this book has been written. To all those I have not mentioned by name, please forgive me and know that you are remembered and cherished.

I feel forever grateful and proud of my immediate family who have lived with this project for so long, suffering and celebrating alongside me, whilst forging their unique, creative lives. Your patience, occasional exasperation and loving encouragement have been vital and essential. To my dear husband Nick, and our four vibrant children, Aaron, Luke, Marigold and Jack, I offer huge love and gratitude.

I acknowledge and give thanks for the hills, mountains, rivers, trees, flowers, birds, animals, stone and rocks of the Cotswolds, the Cambrians, the Himalayas, Pembrokeshire and the Pyrenees. They have given much to sustain and purify the poetic landscape of my mind.

Finally, thank you Lucy. Your life and death have deepened my knowledge of love and grace. After eighteen years our book is ready to leave home, with trust and hope that it will generate more healing, compassion, wisdom and generosity. May it nourish all who depend upon this tender, mysterious planet earth.

Marian Partington, February 2012